Inner Alchemy Astrology

Inner Alchemy Astrology

Practical Techniques for Controlling Your Destiny

Mantak Chia and Christine Harkness-Giles

Destiny Books

Rochester, Vermont • Toronto, Canada

Destiny Books
One Park Street
Rochester, Vermont 05767
www.DestinyBooks.com

Destiny Books is a division of Inner Traditions International

Originally published in Thailand in 2011 by Universal Tao Publications under the title *Inner Alchemy from the Stars: Practical Taoist Astrology*

Library of Congress Cataloging-in-Publication Data
Chia, Mantak, 1944–
  [Inner alchemy from the stars]
  Inner alchemy astrology : practical techniques for controlling your destiny / Mantak Chia and Christine Harkness-Giles.
    p. cm.
  Rev. ed. of: Inner alchemy from the stars : practical Taoist astrology. 2011.
  Includes index.
  Summary: "Strengthen the qualities in your Taoist astrological chart with Inner Alchemy techniques and Universal Healing Tao exercises"—Provided by publisher.
  ISBN 978-1-59477-469-0 (pbk.) — ISBN 978-1-62055-139-4 (e-book)
  1. Taoist astrology. 2. Alchemy—Miscellanea. I. Title.
  BF1714.T34C49 2013
  133.5'949514—dc23
                                                    2012047619

Printed and bound in the United States by Versa Press

10   9   8   7   6   5   4   3   2   1

Text design by Priscilla H. Baker and layout by Virginia Scott Bowman
This book was typeset in Janson Text and Futura with Sho, Futura, Diotima, and Present used as display typefaces

Contents

Acknowledgments

The authors extend our gratitude to the many generations of Taoist masters who have passed on their special lineage in the form of an unbroken oral transmission over thousands of years. We thank Taoist Master Yi Eng (One Cloud Hermit) for his openness in transmitting the formulas of Taoist Inner Alchemy.

We offer our eternal gratitude and love to our parents and teachers for their many gifts to us. Remembering them brings joy and satisfaction to our continued efforts in presenting the concepts and techniques of the Universal Healing Tao System; their contribution has been crucial.

We wish to thank the thousands of unknown men and women of the Taoist healing arts who developed many of the methods and ideas presented in this book. For their continuous personal encouragement, we wish to thank our fellow instructors, Taoists, students, astrology clients, families, and friends who have inspired the writing of this book by their eager desire to understand Inner Alchemy astrology.

Special thanks go to our Thai production team—Hirunyathorn Punsan, Sopitnapa Promnon, Udon Jandee, and Suthisa Chaisam—for their work on the previous edition of this book, as well as many of the images.

Putting Inner Alchemy into Practice

The information presented in this book is based on the authors' personal experiences and knowledge of Taoist astrology and Universal Healing Tao practices. The practices and chart reading described in this book have been used successfully for thousands of years by Taoists trained by personal instruction. However readers should not undertake the practices without receiving personal transmission and training from a certified instructor of the Universal Healing Tao. Certain practices, if done improperly, may cause injury or result in health problems. This book is intended to supplement individual training by the Universal Healing Tao and to serve as a reference guide. Anyone who undertakes these practices on the basis of this book alone does so entirely at his or her own risk.

The meditations, practices, and techniques of astrological interpretation described herein are not intended to be used as an alternative or substitute for professional medical treatment and care. If any readers are suffering from illnesses based on mental or emotional disorders, an appropriate professional health care practitioner or therapist should be consulted. Such problems should be corrected before you start Universal Healing Tao training.

Neither the Universal Healing Tao nor its staff and instructors nor Inner Traditions can be held responsible for the consequences of any practice or misuse of the information contained in this book. If the reader undertakes any exercise without strictly following the instructions, notes, and warnings, the responsibility must lie solely with the reader.

This book does not attempt to give any medical diagnosis, treatment, prescription, or remedial recommendation in relation to any human disease, ailment, suffering, or physical condition whatsoever.

 Introduction

Taoist astrology and Chinese astrology are actually the same thing. Many disciplines of the Taoist arts are referred to as either Chinese or Taoist yet are identical. This is because early Taoist thought was mainly defined in China, and so many of the theories were justifiably "Chinese" at the time.

Chinese astrology defines the five-element makeup of a person using calculations based on the year, month, day, and time of birth. The place of birth has relevance as well—particularly important is to know if daylight saving time was in use at the time of your birth, in which case the hour needs adjusting. Daylight saving time does not show where the natural place of the sun was, and it is solar time and solar year that are used.

Chinese astrology is also known as the Four Pillars of Destiny. The year, month, day, and time information form four "pillars" of information about your life, as defined by the universal energy at the time of birth. It is also called Ba Zi, which means "eight characters," as each of these four pillars has two parts—a heavenly stem and an earthly branch—making eight characters. They are expressed in five-element terms.

Knowledge of your own five-element makeup can help you with your Supreme Inner Alchemy practices, or if you are an instructor, you can use astrological chart information with your students. Knowledge of their own element makeup will help them better understand the principles behind the meditations and the positive and negative emotions stored in their own organs. It will be an aid to achieving faster, more pertinent, and balanced results.

The Universal Healing Tao practices are based on Inner Alchemy, which means changing the balance of elements within yourself. These esoteric practices involve connecting yourself to the original element energies. Therefore, understanding the relative strengths of your own elements can make the practices more personally beneficial. Although your calculated birth (or natal) chart itself will not be changed by the practices, you can balance and strengthen elements within yourself and this can change your health and "fate." Indeed, it is more difficult to read the chart of a long-practicing Taoist as he or she will have already corrected some element weaknesses through Inner Alchemy.

This book is written to accompany calculations from the Taoist or five-element astrology program on Mantak Chia's website: www .universal-tao.com/InnerAlchemyAstrology. The first seven chapters describe how you can use the information from your free Inner Alchemy chart to understand your own five-element makeup and balance it using Inner Alchemy practices. The last three chapters continue with explanations on the dynamic, changing luck cycles and other further interpretations that can be paired with the full personal Inner Alchemy astrology chart also available from the website for a fee. Please note that appendix A contains useful reference tables from throughout the book. Once you have read the book and understand the basics of interpreting your birth chart, you can use this appendix for easy access while working on your own chart interpretations.

This book can also be used with accurate data from self-calculated charts or other Chinese astrology program charts. There are Universal Healing Tao instructors throughout the world who can teach the practices referred to in this book. (Consult www.universal-tao.com, the Universal Healing Tao website, for instructors in your country.) The art of Inner Alchemy astrology is also regularly taught by the authors.

Taoist Astrology

Taoist Supreme Inner Alchemy astrology and feng shui were conceived thousands of years ago from observations that early Taoists made about the constellations above us and how their positions correlated to people and their fates. The only data people had available came from looking at the sky. The astrological chart could then be plotted using the birth data of the person. This system has equivalents in the Indian Ayurvedic system and in the traditional Western system.

Common to both Western and Taoist astrology is a birth-data chart and "luck periods," as they are called in Taoist astrology, which show changes of energy coming toward us as our planets rotate in the cosmos. This makes Taoist astrology a dynamic interpretational method, indicating ever-changing energy patterns. The Taoist Inner Alchemy philosophy also provides ways to change and improve upon the basic birth-chart energy, making Taoist astrology a fascinating interactive tool rather than a static prediction of one's life and fate. Therefore, the special quality of Taoist astrology is the facility to reinforce and harmonize the energies by using Supreme Inner Alchemy practices.

Your astrological chart is an analysis of what you are born with, coming from that first gasp of air; it is a calculation of your five-element makeup. Each of the five elements relates to organs, emotions, sense organs, and types of actions in your life on the level of vibrational chi, or vital energy. The planets move in the heavens; the universe is not static but constantly changing. From your birth data, the metaphysical art of Taoist astrology can also calculate when the energies of the five elements will become stronger or weaker in you.

Energy is dynamic, both inside you and within the universe. For this reason, it is better to look at your astrology chart as indicative of your original energy and incoming energy influences—and therefore something you have the power to work on—rather than a pure reading of your future as if it were your fate and you were helpless to change anything. Astrology can provide a picture of the health of the body and its organs on the day of its birth, but of course how that body is fed, brought up, cared for, and its environment will affect it too. Stress, abuse, and poor living conditions can exaggerate the weaknesses and deficiencies you are born with; equally meditations and correct food and living conditions can help you balance the energy within and greatly improve your life.

Taoist astrology, feng shui, and the divinatory arts all place emphasis on the cosmic trilogy—heaven luck, earth luck, and human luck.

Astrology also adds an interesting dimension to the nature versus nurture debate on raising children. If you wonder why your children are so different from each other, then consult an astrologer as well as a psychologist and geneticist.

Taoist feng shui has a common origin with Taoist astrology inasmuch as these early observations were the base for calculations of the moon and sun rotations. When combined with the front (or facing) and sitting angle of a person's house, feng shui methods then gave indications of prevailing energies and likely interpretable events for the occupants.

Feng shui initially involved the relationship between the burial place of one's ancestors and the person's luck. Known as yin house feng shui, it is still important mainly in Asian countries where ancestor worship is common. Tomb placements were, and still are, chosen to increase good fortune for the descendants. Luck in Chinese society is about wealth, health, and longevity. Although Western society can be coy about personal interest in money, to Chinese society it is just seen as a form of energy with no shame being attached to desiring it. So wealth, or prosperity, accompanied by good health and a life long enough to enjoy it was considered most fortunate.

In the West there is not always much scope for choosing burial sites, and cremation is common in many cultures. Therefore the vast majority of feng shui work here is yang house feng shui, which concerns the place of the living. It involves calculations around the home, shop, or workplace and how the energy there affects one's luck and how it can be improved.

The form school of feng shui came from observations on surrounding landscapes—the mountains, rivers, and lakes around a building and the influence these had on events. It was indeed necessary observation for farming and managing flooding areas, to provide irrigation and to be prepared for the effects of the prevailing winds and seasonal changes. These observations were diligently recorded in order to manage food and essentials. Today this form of feng shui is used to the advantage of multinational companies, many Asian businesses, and for interested individuals. Famous examples are the water and mountain form studies around Hong Kong.

LAW AND ORDER—
WU CHI AND THE PLANETS

These Taoist arts are all based on the law and order of the universe, which is calculated in astronomy.

The moon revolves around the earth; that is a law. It takes twenty-eight and a half days, which is one lunar month. This does not change; the lunar calendar goes back over 4,700 years. The earth revolves around the sun in a constant orbit of 365 and a quarter days. Gravity is the pull that keeps planets orbiting in the same way and that keeps the universe in order—and has done so for five billion

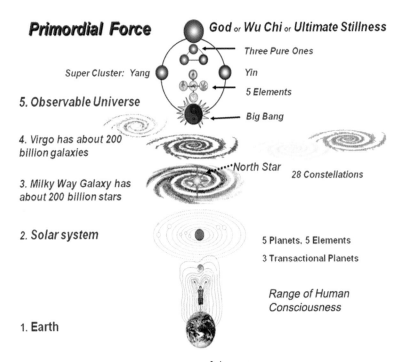

Figure 1.1. Law of the universe—
how the Wu Chi and the planets affect us

years. The plotting of eclipses goes far back. Stonehenge and other prehistoric sites are thought to have been built as observatories or places of celebration to the heavens above. They achieved extraordinary accuracy in relation to cosmic position and events.

Our solar system has eight planets. There are about two hundred billion stars like our own star, the sun, in the galaxy. From our solar system we continue up to the North Star, which controls the earth, sun, planets, and the billions of other stars. Under the laws of the universe, the constellations spin around the North Star and the Southern Cross. It is considered to be a portal to the Wu Chi, or the primordial force that is the beginning of the universe.

Taoists believe that continuing up from the North Star, the five element stars govern the cosmos with their forces. They affect the whole universe, including the earth, everything that is on it, and our

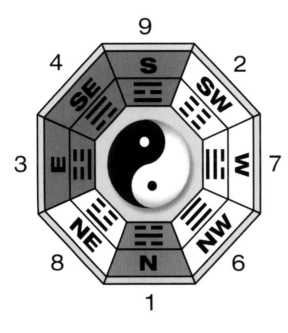

Figure 1.2. Pakua with trigrams and directions and Tai Chi in the center. Note that 5 naturally resides in the center. Unlike Western compasses, Chinese compasses traditionally have south at the top and north at the bottom.

bodies. The Tai Chi symbol in figure 1.1 illustrates this concept as a spinning sphere where there is always at least a seed of yin in the yang and a seed of yang in the yin, as the balance waxes and wanes.

Above the five elements are the Three Pure Ones, and then the Wu Chi—the ultimate stillness—also known as the Supreme Creator or God to religious groups. From the nothingness of Wu Chi creation started, and positive and negative energies emerged, seen as the Tai Chi—the pure yang and the pure yin. This is the Big Bang of science. These two actions gave birth to four states, then six, and then divided again to become the eight trigrams of the *pakua*, which represent the eight forces of the universe. This will be discussed more in chapters 5 and 7.

Note that the unbroken line represents yang, and the broken line represents yin. Trigrams are read starting from the center outward, so we would read the trigram for the south: yang, yin, yang. The trigram for west would be yang, yang, yin. The numbers on the outside are used in flying star feng shui and represent the following:

1	=	Water
2, 5, and 8	=	Earth (5 is in the center)
3 and 4	=	Wood
6 and 7	=	Metal
9	=	Fire

WU XING—FIVE ELEMENTS

Each trigram is made up of three lines of either yin or yang and the five elements are described within the pakua. The name "five elements" comes from the Chinese expression that translates as *wu* (five) and *xing* (the changing states of being). These five energies are best described by the names of the five elements they are given— Fire, Earth, Metal, Water, and Wood. So when we are discussing the five elements in your chart, remember that we are really discussing five types of energy rather than the material of those elements. The balance of these five elements and the yin and yang in a person's makeup have a major bearing on what is beneficial and effective for that person in terms of Supreme Inner Alchemy feng shui. The interpretation of your chart involves understanding how these five energies interact.

The five element stars together govern trillions of stars and billions of galaxies. As they orbit, their influence imbues us—their energies are in us all and everything on the earth. The North Star is the most easily recognizable star in the Northern Hemisphere night sky; it is in a line with the two "pointer" stars of the Big Dipper. The North Star beams down to our planet, together with the influence of the yin and yang and five elements, from the firmament above it. Together with the Southern Cross it governs the earth, whose axis is tilted between the two. Earth is a very small object compared to the other planets. Earth's surface is around 70 percent water, as is the human body. The moon pulls on water, creating high and low tides, and its pull affects crops, body fluids, and menstrual cycles. Knowing this lunar effect you can imagine the effect other larger planets have on us. These forces affect us all of the time in everyday life; calculating and understanding them is astrology.

TAOIST CONCEPT OF TIME

To construct the astrological chart your birth data is "translated" into Taoist time using calculations based on traditional astronomy and calendars. It is in two parts: heavenly stems and earthly branches.

Heavenly Stems

To early Taoists, heaven (or the sky) and time were the same thing. They invented a system to mark time using the five elements, based on the cycle of the seasons of the year and incorporating the yin and yang; it is known as the ten heavenly stems. The ten heavenly stems describe the rotation of time in heaven, seen as a round disc. There is a yin and yang phase of each of the five elements, making ten stems.

Heaven's year starts with spring. Many cultures have celebrations at that time of the year—Carnival, Mardi Gras, Lent—connected with coming out of winter, the equinox, and the start of growth.

Spring is growth; the element is Wood. At the end of spring plants start to burn up in the heat of summer; the element of summer is Fire. After the hottest part of summer there is an Indian summer before autumn; the element of Indian summer is Earth. Indian summer can still be hot when the burnt matter returns to the earth as ashes. This gives way to autumn, as the mineral deposits harden in the earth; the element of autumn is Metal. This leads to winter when the concentration of Metal becomes liquid; the element of winter is Water. The Water feeds the seeds and shriveled plants in the earth, and there is again vegetal growth and spring; the element of spring is Wood, and so goes the cycle.

As the sun rises in the east, so the cycle of heavenly stems starts in the direction of east, following with south, then the center, west, and north. It starts with Yang Wood.

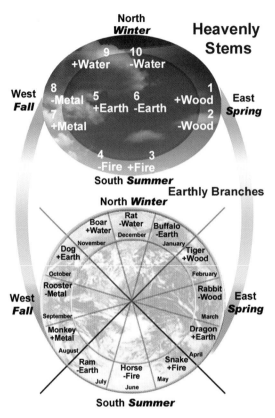

Figure 1.3. The ten heavenly stems meeting the twelve earthly branches

Earthly Branches—Time Measured on Earth

On Earth the beginning of the Chinese year is around February (depending on the moon cycle) when it is still winter. However, the year used in astrology is the solar year, whose new year date varies less.

To distinguish between time in the heavens and time on the earth, there are twelve earthly branches. Their origin is from observations of the orbit of Jupiter, which is approximately twelve years long.

These twelve branches describe not only the twelve months of the year, and therefore the seasons, but also directions and hours. They have the names of twelve animals. The cycle starts in winter with the Rat, followed by Buffalo, Tiger, Rabbit, Dragon, Snake, Horse, Ram, Monkey, Rooster, Dog, and Boar (see figure 1.3). Note that there are variants in the animal names used by Chinese astrologers. Ram is sometimes called

Sheep, Boar is Pig, Buffalo is Ox, Rooster is Cock, and Rabbit is Cat. The characteristics associated with the animals remain the same.

Each branch-hour represents a time block of two hours in the twenty-four-hour day. The energy of their time often displays characteristics of the animals. For example, the Rat is a nocturnal animal and it begins the cycle; Rat hour is 11 p.m. to 1 a.m. (2300–0100 hrs.). So the new day starts halfway through Rat hour.

The year was divided into twenty-four periods, beginning around February 4—the new solar year—when the Big Dipper points east and the sun enters 15° Aquarius. There is a precise time that changes for each year; for 1924 it was 9:45 a.m. (0945 hrs.) on February 5.

The heavenly stems are constantly coming to Earth to interact with the forces here. So the ten heavenly stems and the twelve earthly branches are paired together to make a cycle of sixty. Each animal is combined once with all five elements, so after counting to sixty we get back to the first one, Wood Rat. Wood is the heavenly stem and Rat the earthly branch.

Note that Earth energy starts with winter, the Rat. In figure 1.3 on the earthly branches cycle you can see that the Rat's energy is Yin Water. The heavenly stems cycle starts with spring (Yang Wood). So the first paired energy of the sixty-year cycle is Yang Wood Rat, which combines the energies of Yang Wood and Yin Water.

SIXTY-YEAR CYCLE OF STEMS AND BRANCHES

(TWO COMPLETE SIXTY-YEAR CYCLES FROM 1924 TO 2043. THE ACTUAL DAY AND TIME OF DAY THAT THE YEAR STARTS VARY.)

	60-YEAR CYCLE YEARS 1924–1983	HEAVENLY STEM	EARTHLY BRANCH	60-YEAR CYCLE 1984–2043
1	Feb 05 1924	Yang Wood	Rat	1984
2	Feb 04 1925	Yin Wood	Buffalo	1985
3	Feb 04 1926	Yang Fire	Tiger	1986
4	Feb 05 1927	Yin Fire	Rabbit	1987
5	Feb 05 1928	Yang Earth	Dragon	1988

	60-YEAR CYCLE YEARS 1924–1983	HEAVENLY STEM	EARTHLY BRANCH	60-YEAR CYCLE 1984–2043
6	Feb 04 1929	Yin Earth	Snake	1989
7	Feb 04 1930	Yang Metal	Horse	1990
8	Feb 05 1931	Yin Metal	Ram	1991
9	Feb 05 1932	Yang Water	Monkey	1992
10	Feb 04 1933	Yin Water	Rooster	1993
11	Feb 04 1934	Yang Wood	Dog	1994
12	Feb 05 1935	Yin Wood	Boar	1995
13	Feb 05 1936	Yang Fire	Rat	1996
14	Feb 04 1937	Yin Fire	Buffalo	1997
15	Feb 04 1938	Yang Earth	Tiger	1998
16	Feb 05 1939	Yin Earth	Rabbit	1999
17	Feb 05 1940	Yang Metal	Dragon	2000
18	Feb 04 1941	Yin Metal	Snake	2001
19	Feb 04 1942	Yang Water	Horse	2002
20	Feb 05 1943	Yin Water	Ram	2003
21	Feb 05 1944	Yang Wood	Monkey	2004
22	Feb 04 1945	Yin Wood	Rooster	2005
23	Feb 04 1946	Yang Fire	Dog	2006
24	Feb 04 1947	Yin Fire	Boar	2007
25	Feb 05 1948	Yang Earth	Rat	2008
26	Feb 04 1949	Yin Earth	Buffalo	2009
27	Feb 04 1950	Yang Metal	Tiger	2010
28	Feb 04 1951	Yin Metal	Rabbit	2011
29	Feb 05 1952	Yang Water	Dragon	2012
30	Feb 04 1953	Yin Water	Snake	2013
31	Feb 04 1954	Yang Wood	Horse	2014
32	Feb 04 1955	Yin Wood	Ram	2015
33	Feb 05 1956	Yang Fire	Monkey	2016

	60-YEAR CYCLE YEARS 1924–1983	HEAVENLY STEM	EARTHLY BRANCH	60-YEAR CYCLE 1984–2043
34	Feb 04 1957	Yin Fire	Rooster	2017
35	Feb 04 1958	Yang Earth	Dog	2018
36	Feb 04 1959	Yin Earth	Boar	2019
37	Feb 05 1960	Yang Metal	Rat	2020
38	Feb 04 1961	Yin Metal	Buffalo	2021
39	Feb 04 1962	Yang Water	Tiger	2022
40	Feb 04 1963	Yin Water	Rabbit	2023
41	Feb 05 1964	Yang Wood	Dragon	2024
42	Feb 04 1965	Yin Wood	Snake	2025
43	Feb 04 1966	Yang Fire	Horse	2026
44	Feb 04 1967	Yin Fire	Ram	2027
45	Feb 05 1968	Yang Earth	Monkey	2028
46	Feb 04 1969	Yin Earth	Rooster	2029
47	Feb 04 1970	Yang Metal	Dog	2030
48	Feb 04 1971	Yin Metal	Boar	2031
49	Feb 05 1972	Yang Water	Rat	2032
50	Feb 04 1973	Yin Water	Buffalo	2033
51	Feb 04 1974	Yang Wood	Tiger	2034
52	Feb 04 1975	Yin Wood	Rabbit	2035
53	Feb 05 1976	Yang Fire	Dragon	2036
54	Feb 04 1977	Yin Fire	Snake	2037
55	Feb 04 1978	Yang Earth	Horse	2038
56	Feb 04 1979	Yin Earth	Ram	2039
57	Feb 05 1980	Yang Metal	Monkey	2040
58	Feb 04 1981	Yin Metal	Rooster	2041
59	Feb 04 1982	Yang Water	Dog	2042
60	Feb 04 1983	Yin Water	Boar	2043

Your birth data is translated into these stems and branches. The top line of your birth chart shows the heavenly stems and the more visible things in our lives. Heaven's energy comes down on us rapidly and easily. The bottom lines of your birth chart are made up of the earthly branches, also referred to as "roots," which show the more buried and deeper part of us. Earth's energy comes up and affects us more slowly and is even more complicated.

FIVE ELEMENTS AND THE RELATIONSHIP BETWEEN THEM

To usefully understand your astrological chart, you must understand how the five elements interact with each other. They are commonly drawn in a pentagon with Fire at the top but the chi flow is shown as a circle in figure 1.4.

We have described the cycle of the seasons earlier in this chapter (see figure 1.3). That cycle is known as the generating cycle, as each element generates or feeds the next one, as in figure 1.4.

There are three important cycles that describe the relationships between the five elements. The relationships are often explained using

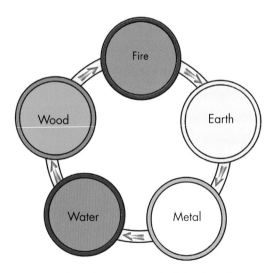

Figure 1.4. Cycle (or Pentagon) of the five elements

a family parallel—a useful image that we will refer to later when analyzing your own chart.

1. Generating Cycle: This goes in the direction Fire, Earth, Metal, Water, Wood, Fire, Earth, and so on. Each element feeds the next one: Fire feeds Earth, Earth feeds Metal, Metal feeds Water, and the pattern continues. The parent feeds the child, therefore the element following in this direction is considered the child.

2. Weakening Cycle: This goes in the opposite direction—Fire, Wood, Water, Metal, Earth, Fire, Wood, and so on. Imagine the arrows in figure 1.4 going in the opposite direction. Alternatively, imagine that the feeding element is weakened by the feeding it is doing. Fire weakens Wood, Wood weakens Water, Water weakens Metal, and so forth. The parent element is weakened by giving to the next element, as it takes energy for a mother to feed her baby, or children can take energy from their parents.

3. Controlling Cycle: Each element controls the element after the element that follows it and is in turn controlled by the element before the one preceding it. Fire controls Metal, Metal controls Wood, Wood controls Earth, Earth controls Water, Water controls Fire. Note that Fire melts Metal when it controls it, Metal cuts Wood, Wood depletes Earth, Earth dries up Water, and Water quenches or extinguishes Fire (see figure 1.5). Using the family image, we call the controller the grandparent and the element controlled the grandchild. For example, in the Fire-controls-Metal relationship, Fire is the grandparent and Metal is the grandchild. Fire's grandparent is Water.

The controlling cycle in reverse gives another weakening cycle inasmuch as holding on to control is tiring. When an element is controlling another one it is effectively weakened, but the sizes of the elements decide on how weakening this would be. Ancient Chinese texts on astrology talked about "insulting" as the opposite reaction to control, a sort of antagonism.

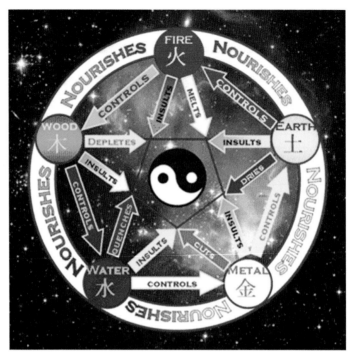

Figure 1.5. Controlling, generating, and
weakening cycles of the five elements

The importance of each of the five elements is equal and they are interdependent. They have an influence over your life and the major organs in your body. If they are out of balance, your astrological chart will tell you, although you will have already noticed the effects. It is helpful to know that you can harmonize the elements by using the Supreme Inner Alchemy practices.

HEAVEN, EARTH, AND HUMAN LUCK

The cosmic trinity describes our destiny.

Heaven luck is what you are born with, as shown in your astrological chart; the first part of the chart, the static birth chart, and the dynamic luck cycles are all determined at your birth.

Earth luck is the environment we live in. We control this to some extent when it is possible for us to live in clean air and without too

Figure 1.6. Cosmic trinity: Heaven luck is defined by what the universe gave us at our birth and the changing energies defined in the time cycles. Earth luck surrounds us, and human luck we make for ourselves. Yet all three interconnect.

much stress. It is also the feng shui of our home or workplace; external feng shui is about the energies of the place and external to our body. In China, good feng shui was considered more important for children than sending them to the right school. Environmental energy will change things for us also; some people live near terrible natural or manmade health hazards. City air can put poisonous lead into the bloodstream of children at a vulnerable age in their development.

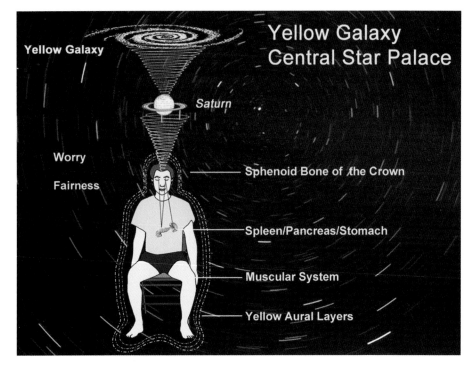

Figure 1.7. Man's connection to earth energy

Human luck is made up of the decisions we make, or the actions we choose. Of course our ability to make good decisions may depend on our astrology and also the luck that our feng shui brings us.

In reality these three things are interdependent as our ability to make good decisions will be affected by our astrological chart. Our clarity, motivation, and the flow of good luck could also depend on our feng shui. How we deal with heaven's luck can be affected by Taoist practices.

Looking at our astrology we see that we have the power to bring more personal harmony into our lives.

Getting to Know Your Chart

Calculations for both astrology and feng shui are very valuable but extremely complicated. Thankfully, it is not necessary to learn how to do them for yourself at this level. Computer programs offer us welcome shortcuts. The first step in finding your Inner Alchemy makeup is to access the website with the chart-making program. The website is found at: www.universal-tao.com/InnerAlchemyAstrology/. All you need to do is enter the year, month, day, and time of your birth—adjusted according to whether there was daylight saving time in your country on that day, which you can look up on the internet if you do not know. These are the four pillars that form your astrological chart.

Astrology and feng shui calculations are based on the Chinese solar year, which starts between February 3 and 5 depending on the year. Because of the slight variation in start date, people with birthdays between the January 1 and February 5 have often been looking at the wrong Chinese year or "animal" for themselves. Our program will automatically obtain the correct Chinese year you were born in. This is different from the lunar new year, which is celebrated as "Chinese New Year" with dragon and lion dances, firecrackers, special food, and little red envelopes containing money; the lunar new year usually falls between January 21 and February 20.

If you do not know the time of day that you were born then you cannot access the information of the fourth pillar (read from right to left; it is the hour pillar—the time of your birth). In that case estimate using what you know and realize that there could be an inaccuracy on that pillar. Possible indicators of your time of birth are also whether you are a "morning" person or "night" person. Someone born in the night usually feels more awake late in the evening or even in the early hours than someone born in the day, who might be an "early bird" type. You could try doing two different charts to see the difference between 2 p.m. (1400 hrs.) and 2 a.m. (0200 hrs.), for example, to give yourself an idea of what difference this information makes overall. However, the most important information for you is on the other three pillars. Your day, month, and year must be accurate to be able to read your astrological chart.

This chart is your astrological birth chart, expressed in the yin and yang of the five elements. It represents the energy that you were born with. This energy can be interpreted in terms of health, wealth, emotions, personality, the family around you, and your interaction with society and the environment. To make interpretations for yourself, the minimum knowledge you need is an understanding of the five elements and yin and yang.

The following table, figure 2.2a, is an example of part of an astrological chart similar to the chart you will get from the website.

	HOUR	DAY	MONTH	YEAR
Stem	Yang Water	Yin Earth	Yin Water	Yin Fire
Branch	Monkey	Buffalo	Buffalo	Ram
	Yang Metal	Yin Earth	Yin Earth	Yin Earth
	Yang Earth	Yin Water	Yin Water	Yin Fire
	Yang Water	Yin Metal	Yin Metal	Yin Wood

Figure 2.2a. Natasha: Female, Born on
January 20, 1968, at 3:10 p.m. (1510 hrs.)

As we saw in chapter 1, the animals are the twelve earthly branches that Taoists use to count time. Each earthly branch has an animal and a main element, but some also have one or two minor elements. These extra minor elements are referred to as hidden roots; there are some schools of astrology that calculate more hidden roots. You will find the animal's elements beneath the animal in the earthly branch line of your birth chart. More about the animals and the relationships between them is found in chapter 9 (to see which elements correspond with each animal see table on page 113).

The program will also translate the above data to give you a breakdown of your elemental makeup; in figure 2.2b we have expressed it in percentages to give you a better idea.

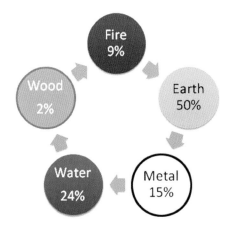

Figure 2.2b. This represents the percentages Natasha has of each of the five elements, from her birth chart in figure 2.2a.

FIND YOUR DAY MASTER

The first thing to do with your chart is find your day master, so called because it is from the day pillar. It is the upper heavenly stem part; it is also the element that represents you. Find your day master and refer to the part of the program where you will see your five-element composition expressed in circles. Examine your day master element and you will see if it is strong or weak; the size of the bubbles and corresponding percentages indicate the strength of the elements. Look also at the element bubble preceding your day master: this is what nourishes you, and so a strong element here will make your day master stronger.

In Natasha's chart looking under day and the upper line, we see that she is an Earth day master—Yin Earth. From the bubble diagram, figure 2.2b, we can see that at 50 percent she has a high percentage of Earth element and we would refer to her as a strong Earth person. The element nourishing her is Fire, which is not very strong. This is less problematic for Natasha because her own self, her Earth element, is powerful.

	HOUR	DAY	MONTH	YEAR
Stem	Yin Wood	Yin Fire	Yin Metal	Yang Earth
Branch	Snake	Rooster	Rooster	Monkey
	Yang Fire	Yin Metal	Yin Metal	Yang Metal
	Yang Earth			Yang Earth
	Yang Metal			Yang Water

Figure 2.3a. Pilar: Female, Born on September 24, 1968, at 9:40 a.m. (0940 hrs.)

Pilar is a Yin Fire person, but unlike Natasha her day master is not the largest element. However, her Metal element is very large.

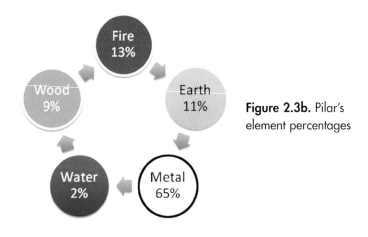

Figure 2.3b. Pilar's element percentages

	HOUR	DAY	MONTH	YEAR
Stem	Yang Metal	Yang Metal	Yin Earth	Yin Wood
Branch	Dragon	Tiger	Buffalo	Snake
	Yang Earth	Yang Wood	Yin Earth	Yang Fire
	Yin Wood	Yang Fire	Yin Water	Yang Earth
	Yin Water	Yang Earth	Yin Metal	Yang Metal

Figure 2.4a. Edward: Male,
Born on January 31, 1966, at 7:00 a.m. (0700 hrs.)

Edward is a very strong Yang Metal day master; you can see that his self element is large and is well nourished by the very large Earth element.

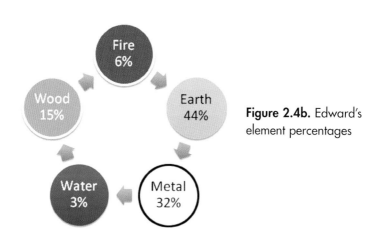

Figure 2.4b. Edward's element percentages

ANALYSIS OF YOUR ORGAN HEALTH

The five elements have corresponding negative and positive emotions, and this energy is stored in the corresponding organs in the body. Having a very strong or very weak element could manifest itself in physical problems in the element organ or a tendency to suffer from the negative emotions assigned to the element. The associations between the elements, emotions, and organs are described in the table below. This table will be used throughout the book and appears in appendix A together with other important tools and tables for your easy reference.

FIVE ELEMENTS, EMOTIONS, AND ORGANS

	FIRE	EARTH	METAL	WATER	WOOD
Yin Organ	Heart	Spleen	Lungs	Kidneys	Liver
Yang Organ	Small Intestines	Pancreas, Stomach	Large Intestine	Bladder	Gallbladder
Sense Organ	Tongue	Mouth, Lips	Nose	Ears	Eyes
Body Parts and Tissues	Blood Circulation System	Armpits, Inner Arms, Muscles	Chest, Skin	Bones, Sexual Organs	Tendons
Positive Emotions	Love, Joy, Happiness, Sincerity	Fairness, Openness, Trust, Justice	Courage, Righteousness	Gentleness, Willpower, Alertness	Generosity, Kindness, Self-Confidence
Negative Emotions	Arrogance, Hastiness, Cruelty, Impatience	Worry, Anxiety	Sadness, Grief, Depression	Fear, Phobias	Anger, Aggression, Jealousy, Envy, Frustration
Color	Red, Purple	Yellow, Beige, Brown	White, Gold, Metal	Black, Dark Blue	Green, Light Blue
Season	Summer	Indian Summer	Fall/Autumn	Winter	Spring
Direction	South	Center	West	North	East
Taste	Bitter	Sweet	Spicy	Salty	Sour
Energy	Radiating	Stabilizing	Contracting	Gathering	Growing
Shape	Triangle	Square	Round	Wavy Lines, Running Lines	Vertical Rectangle
Planet	Mars	Saturn	Venus	Mercury	Jupiter

We will look at the organ health energy for our three examples—Natasha, Pilar, and Edward.

Natasha (figures 2.2a and 2.2b)

From her birth chart information Natasha would have a weak liver, gallbladder, heart, and small intestines. She would have normal lungs, large intestines, kidneys, and bladder. In astrology "more" does not necessarily mean better. Excess can cause as many problems as lack. So her very strong spleen, stomach, and pancreas could be a source of problems or perhaps vulnerability.

She would be very suited to working with or managing other people. She would be serious, caring, and dependable. Emotionally, we could expect her to worry a lot; fairness would always be an issue for her; she could also suffer from the negative emotions stored in her liver and heart, which are weak and more vulnerable to stress, frustration, and impatience. As many Taoist practices are about balancing the energies to bring about harmony, there is opportunity for Natasha to benefit from a chart with such highs and lows of energies. Exceptionally strong elements can denote exceptional lives.

Pilar (figures 2.3a and 2.3b)

We could expect Pilar to be a passionate person, well-paid, and capable of making good, rapid decisions on important matters. She is capable of great achievements. Her weaker organs would be her kidneys, bladder, liver, and gallbladder. Her very strong lungs and large intestines need some balancing; she could suffer from skin problems. She is very courageous, tenacious, and to the point. Her very strong Metal energy could be usefully brought around to help her other organs during the Inner Smile meditation, which will be discussed in chapter 5.

Edward (figures 2.4a and 2.4b)

Although Edward is a Metal person, he is also very earthy and organized. His weaker organs would be his kidneys, bladder, heart, and small intestines. Emotionally he is likely to suffer most from fear and impatience. By using his strong Earth resource energy, he could strengthen his Water and Fire energy during the Inner Smile meditation.

Now you can identify the basic parts of your chart: your five elements and their strengths, including your day master, as well as your branch animals and elements. How to apply Taoist practices to balance the elements in your astrological chart is explained in chapter 5. The sections on ten-year luck cycles will be covered in chapter 8. In the next chapter we will explore the ten types of day masters and what they mean for you.

Ten Types of Day Masters

There are ten types of day master, one for each of the yin and yang of the five elements. In this chapter we offer descriptions and common personality traits of each of these types and how they might affect you. We also discuss how you can tell the strength of your day master, which has implications for how accurate these descriptions will seem. The self-awareness that comes from examining your day master can also help in your career. By knowing your day master you can see how appropriate your chosen career is or, if you long for a different life, how much the new career would be suited to you. Careers are discussed near the end of this chapter.

We have discussed what each of the five elements represents, and what the concepts of yin and yang mean, but what do they mean in terms of your day master? We could refer to the yang version as the "big" version of the element and the yin version as the "small" one. For example, Yang Wood can be seen as trees, while Yin Wood is more like plants, houseplants, and shrubs.

However, that does not mean that big is better. They are different—as are yin and yang—and are suitable in different situations. Another way to express the difference is that the yin version is more "subtle" and the yang version more "direct." Imagine them as in the picture images given below.

Figure 3.1. Yang Wood—large trees

Figure 3.2. Yin Wood—plants, houseplants, and shrubs

Figure 3.3. Yang Fire—a big fire, the sun

Figure 3.4. Yin Fire—a candle, a lamp

Figure 3.5. Yang Earth—mountain, a large quantity
of earth, a big dam

Figure 3.6. Yin
Earth—the earth in a
plant pot

Figure 3.7. Yang Metal—a sword

Figure 3.8. Yin Metal—jewelry

Figure 3.9. Yang Water—a large lake, river

Figure 3.10. Yin Water—a glass of water, light rain

Although one is larger than the other, they each have their own strengths and characteristics while sharing the behavior of the element. Take Metal people: Yang Metal people are fast to act, going straight for the action on their own if necessary; they are often of leader mentality and do not wait to be told what to do. Yin Metal people are more subtle and although also decision makers; they can probably wait to read instructions and listen to advice. Yang Metal is more cutting; in speech this can come over as brutally blunt. It is the difference between the sword and gold jewelry. Keep these distinguishing factors in mind as you read about your day master.

CHARACTERISTICS OF YOUR DAY MASTER

These are descriptions of the ten day masters' personality traits. However, your day master strength together with the quantity and quality of the other four elements in your natal chart will affect how much of it applies to you. Incoming timely energies will also affect your day master and will be described in chapter 8.

Yang Wood Day Master

Yang Wood is the energy of the large tree: strong, powerful, steady, forthright, direct, stern, down-to-earth, straightforward, sturdy, stubborn, unbending, reliable, supportive, outspoken, determined, righteous, honorable, deep-rooted, and serious. At work, Yang Wood is professional with a keen sense of responsibility. Planning and vision are strong points, together with an ability to see a project through to the end, like a tree reaching upward toward sunlight.

Yang Wood day masters have strong willpower, not giving up easily in the face of adversity; their reputation and morals are an important issue for them. They are sympathetic to those in need of help but authoritarian, bossy, predictable, slow-witted, and slow to change or compromise. They can be stiff and thick-skinned when it comes to understanding what is happening around them, giving the impression that they are uncaring.

Yin Wood Day Master

Yin Wood is vegetation like flowers and plants; soft, weak, meek, and mild, but flexible, adaptable, fickle, expressive, extroverted, charismatic, creative, manipulative, quick-witted, possessive, careful, and good with money. Yin Wood day masters are survivors, good motivators, and good project leaders.

Yin Wood finds its way in life like the shoots that eventually reach the sunlight at the top of the forest canopy.

Yin Wood day masters know how to skirt around trouble but can be timid, easily swayed, and change their minds and strategy easily according to circumstances.

With a tendency to hold grudges, they may be easily deceived or mislead, give way to temptation, lose confidence quickly. But if well rooted, they can survive a storm easier than Yang Wood.

Yang Fire Day Master

Yang Fire is like the sun, it radiates warmth and light; it can be generous, open, sincere, just, upright, noble, vibrant, explosive, passionate, independent, outgoing, selfish, lonely, arrogant, opinionated, charismatic, straightforward, relentless, and bossy. Born leaders and warriors, Yang Fire day masters are good talkers but not always good listeners.

Expressive and sentimental, Yang Fire day masters will take up a cause with vigor; they like routines but get bored easily or become impatient.

These sun kings can think the world revolves around them. Although they can help others, they can lose support through their impatience. They can be conceited and impatient in actions, speech, and ideas, leading to misunderstandings. They have a tendency to waste resources and suffer from mood swings and bad tempers. They need to keep their flames under control to achieve their maximum potential.

Yin Fire Day Master

Yin Fire is glowing moonlight and candles; it is mild, gentle, adventurous, diplomatic, private, conservative, courteous, warm, deep, careful, cautious, unhurried, and pays attention to detail in contrast to the hotter Yang Fire.

Yin Fire day masters are sentimental, inspirational, motivating, giving, good friends, sensitive, tolerant, dependable, good motivators, born leaders, and good performers. They are fast thinkers, taking pride in leading and illuminating others and in careful planning.

They can be fickle but know how to rise to an occasion with endurance and energy. They are easily demotivated and do not always communicate their feelings or their plans and actions, which tends to irritate others.

Yang Earth Day Master

Yang Earth is like a high mountain or deep earth.

Yang Earth people are very protective; they can be counted on as friends. They are trustworthy, loyal, caring, dependable, solid, optimistic, stubborn, steady, broad-minded, honest, fair, unwavering, inflexible, immovable, stable, self-respecting, and willful, with their feet on the ground.

Yang Earth day masters will look after their foundations: the earth under their feet and other people. They can be slow to gain momentum but do not lose sight of their goal. Their consistency and high notions of justice are inspiring for others and they have good social and organizational skills. They get down to the nitty-gritty at work and do not waste time on talking.

However, their inflexibility and their chronic worrying can compromise their projects.

Yin Earth Day Master

Yin Earth is the moist soil from field and garden; if this earth is wet it can easily be washed away in the rains.

The Yin Earth day master has a high level of understanding and learning; their grasp of knowledge is rapid, they are intellectually versatile with a soft, flexible, comfortable nature. They will inspire confidence to handle difficult problems.

Good at managing and nurturing people, they are tolerant, productive, hardworking, resourceful, innovative, creative, sensitive, caring, usually good-hearted, dependable, and permanently driven to improve themselves. With their strong sense of justice they have an understanding of others' weaknesses and failings.

They can lack adaptability and show poor ability to make quick, spontaneous decisions. Worry can disable their projects and concentration levels, leaving room for rashness at times or compromise on decisions taken. Sometimes they are taken for granted by others.

Yang Metal Day Master

Yang Metal is the strong and powerful metal that can be made into swords or other weapons. It is tough, driven, selfless, righteous, stubborn, direct, sharp, tenacious, determined, loyal, strong-willed, quick-witted, and does not like admitting to failure.

Yang Metal day masters have endurance and stamina and can tolerate hardship and suffering to achieve their goals, with hands-on methods. They know how to build a team, communicate, and analyze a situation.

They can lack flexibility of thought and attention to detail, and can be hasty in action. They show enthusiasm and determination in whatever they do, but they may not always express their inner feelings to others, appearing withdrawn. Their dislike of hypocrisy, unfairness, and untruths means that their remarks can be cuttingly blunt to others, making enemies easily.

Yin Metal Day Master

Yin Metal is gold and the fine metals of jewelry. It is beautiful, gentle, sensitive, attention-seeking, sentimental, easily approachable, helpful, expressive, egocentric, opinionated, confident, sharp, driven, quick-thinking, moral, attractive, interested in appearances, and sociable.

Yin Metal day masters value relationships, but they can take things like money at face value. They have fine feelings, unique opinions, big hearts, and are generous. They want the best. They make good friends, but they are often on show and seek the limelight. They love the new, the beautiful, the latest, so they can seem vain. Their condensing energy means that they like to collect, to store, to put in the bank; indeed they are good bankers, good decision-makers, and good with money. They have relentless energy for work and projects.

Yang Water Day Master

Yang Water is the ocean, lake, river, or turbulent water. Yang Water day masters are intelligent, clean, adaptable, gentle, soft-hearted, enthusiastic, likable, extroverted, rebellious, good communicators, forceful, intuitive, persevering, sociable, noticeable, determined, resourceful, impatient, and always on the move with great, sometimes violent energy.

They love adventure and physical activity; they flow around obstacles, neglecting comfort, grasping the right opportunities, showing little signs of worry as they surf toward their goal. Their fluid path can lead to many distractions from the task in hand as they lose focus on their objectives. They are philosophical and freedom-loving and feel discomfort when restrained. Fear can let them down.

Yin Water Day Master

Yin Water is soft, gentle moisture like the rain or dew. It is peaceful, diligent, hardworking, imaginative, adaptable, introverted, clean, honest, down-to-earth, steady, calm, thinking, intuitive, philosophical, likable, creative, and a good teacher or communicator.

Yin Water day masters do not sit still for long. They can be cool, clear-headed, and sensitive to others' feelings but don't manage their own feelings well, tending to keep things private. They commonly harbor fantasies and romantic thoughts. They value principles and can see the greater good. They are led by their hearts when pursuing careers or dreams.

They can have poor staying power, be nervous, fearful, or even phobic.

DOES YOUR CAREER FIT YOUR DAY MASTER ELEMENT?

Each of the five elements has defining characteristics and most readers will have already found a career in a field that relates to their day master. Descriptions and compatible careers for the five elements follow. However, it is never as simple as making five titles and giving lists below them of suitable careers. Articles in magazines that divide the world's population into four or five groups according to the shape of their nose, blood group, or other criteria can never be anything other than approximate generalizations, whatever the theory behind them.

The Taoist astrology describing individuals is almost as complex as their DNA. If two completely identical charts were found then we could not ignore the environment and circumstances of the people's lives; those variables would show up in the differences in their lives. Heaven luck, earth luck, and human luck are always interlinked. The lists must be interpreted according to the strength of your day master and of other strong elements in your makeup, the incoming element of the cycles of time, and of course your own earthly environment.

If you do not find yourself in a career defined by your element as below and you have frustrations around your work, then you might find more harmony by changing to something that fits in better with your day master and chart. If you are a weak day master and there is an obviously dominating "other" element in your chart, then you would also be drawn toward something in that element's compatible career list. You may also be successful or drawn to a career defined by your wealth element as discussed in chapter 4.

Note that actually using the material of the element could be suitable as a career, but it is really the energy of the element needed to do a certain job that is relevant. As an example, for Wood people carpentry and wood sculpturing would be obviously suitable, and wooden structures would be a good investment; but there is also an organized, verbal energy that would be good for lawyers, a competitive streak for salespeople, and an empathy with plants that would make working with herbs interesting.

Energy required for some careers within the wood industry might fit in more with other day master elements. The energy of a salesperson could involve the skills and love of performing of the Fire element, the communication and speaking of the Water element, the negotiation and decision-making of the Metal element, and you could even argue for the trust and stability of the Earth element. When looking at your career satisfaction you might see where your weak elements leave you out of your comfort zone for certain tasks.

> **Wood People:** Positive emotions are kindness and generosity; the energy is upward growth and expansion. Strong tempers and frustrations can prevail, as the negative emotions stored in the liver are anger, frustration, envy, jealousy, and stress. They are extroverted, sociable, not often alone, and enjoy seeing a project through to its finish. They can handle pressure and see the greater scheme or future of a plan. They can get irritated by

people around them if they are not doing things exactly as prescribed. Although susceptible to stress, they can handle a lot of pressure. Wood is the growing spring energy from the east.

Wood People Careers: Writing, publishing, book-related lines of work, herbs, plants, woodwork, education, accountancy, law, planning, teaching.

Fire People: Positive emotions are love, joy, happiness; the energy is radiating. Strong Fire people might be easily explosive or temperamental. Other negative emotions stored in the heart are hastiness and impatience, but often accompanied by charisma. They love performing. Passion, excitement, and flamboyance make them adventurous and ready for the new; they are project leaders, good warriors, and can be arrogant. Fire people can illuminate and bring light to a situation. They need to keep those flames under control to achieve. Fire energy is from the south, the energy of summer.

Fire People Careers: Electronics, computers, and electrics (considered "fire"), power plants, performing—acting, selling, giving lectures, restaurants, food and drink industries, munitions.

Earth People: Positive emotions are stability, fairness, notions of justice, caring, trustworthiness; this is the energy of our Earth, feet on the ground, down-to-earth. Their sense of justice can bring chronic worry, which is the major negative emotion stored in the spleen. They are steady, consistent, sensitive, and reliable; they can manage people and plans well. They take their time and take precautions when stepping out; they like their changing situations to be organized properly. They get down to the nitty-gritty and do not waste time with too much talking; they can also be stubborn and rigid in their thinking. Earth is the stabilizing energy of the center, of the Indian summer and in-between seasons.

Earth People Careers: Real estate, building and construction, clay work, mining, farming, magistrates, management, organization, consultants, dealing with people—human resources, planning, the "caring" professions.

Metal People: Positive emotions are motivation, courage, and righteousness; the energy is conserving, gathering. Decisions come quickly to both Yin and Yang Metal; they can be very driven, follow goals tenaciously, are sharp and can have a tendency not to involve others in decisions. But they are good at grouping people together efficiently. At work they can communicate the important efficiently, but in their personal lives they are deeply reflective and will not always express their inner selves, making them appear withdrawn, isolated, and even loners. Negative emotions stored in the lungs are sadness, depression, and grief. Metal is the contracting energy from the west, the energy of autumn.

Metal People Careers: Steel, gold, the metallurgy industries, jewelry, cars, planes. Also fields that involve strategy, analysis, and rapid decision making, banking, stock market, trading.

Water People: Positive emotions are intelligence, expression, freedom, gentleness, and caring. Their energy runs and flows. This can show itself as flexible and adaptable but also wandering away from the task in hand, being diverted, and losing focus. They are very intuitive, flexible, and persevering; in projects they stand a good chance of success as they can adapt their methods to what is happening around them. Water can flow around an obstacle, so taking an indirect path comes naturally. They communicate well; they can both express their ideas and listen to others. Fear is the major negative emotion stored in the kidneys. Water is the flowing energy from the north, the energy of winter.

Water People Careers: Boats, ships, fishing, transport, cleaning, communication, advertising, publicity, sales, teaching, healing, medicine, massage (but needs strong Fire element too), spiritual fields, philosophers.

IS YOUR DAY MASTER STRONG OR WEAK?

We have already started referring to a "weak" or a "strong" day master; it is one of the first things to establish.

Astrology calculations are based on dates that are then codified into Chinese celestial language. All of that mathematical work is necessary before we can even begin to learn how to analyze the chart; it is of course the interpretation that is so interesting and a real art.

Here the program provides you with what you need. It is a calculation involving the number of times that the element appears in the chart, the "timeliness" of the element, and how much it is "fed" by its parent. Deductions are then made for the strength of its weakening elements.

You can work out whether your day master is considered to be weak, very weak, normal, strong, or very strong based on the percentage bubbles and the corresponding strengths of the other four elements. This is also included on your Universal Tao Inner Alchemy astrology chart.

THE TIMELINESS OF
THE DAY MASTER ELEMENT

As we follow the cycle of elements and the seasons, each of these five elements is at a developing stage according to the month and season of your birth. Take the example of day master Metal: that means the person was born on a Metal day as shown by the day pillar heavenly stem. But if the birth month pillar is in the spring, Metal is in a trapped state; in the summer it is considered inactive. During the Indian summer it is ready to be very strong—or timely—during its own autumn season when it is robust and vibrant, and then weaker again during winter.

Imagine the element as a plant that comes from a seed in the ground, pushes up, grows, flowers, then withers and dies away where it remains until the seed will start to come to life again. Now imagine this for plants that blossom at differing seasons to explain the five elements' strongest point in their blooming season.

4

Your Five-Element Makeup

Now that you have explored the characteristics of your day master element, or your "self," let's look at the roles of the other four elements. What do they mean to you? They each represent an important part of your life, the types of action in your life, commonly called "phases" in astrology. The role of each element is determined by its relationship to your day master element.

Follow the order of the elements arranged in the pentagon comprising the five element bubbles, in the generating cycle direction. Your day master is your **self/friends**, the one after your day master is your **expression**, then **wealth**, then **power,** and finally the one preceding your day master is your **resource**.

Look again at our first three examples. We have put in the phases according to the elements, starting with the day master. Then look at the five phases of your own bubble chart.

Three Previous Examples

Natasha's expression element is Metal, her wealth is Water, power/ husband element is Wood, and her resource is Fire. Earth represents her self, her friends, and her competitors.

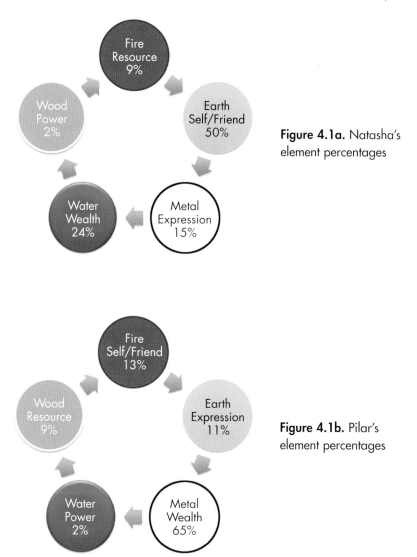

Figure 4.1a. Natasha's element percentages

Figure 4.1b. Pilar's element percentages

Pilar's expression element is Earth, her wealth is Metal, her power/husband is Water, her resource is Wood, and her self, friends, and competitors element is Fire.

Edward's expression element is Water, his wealth/wife is Wood, his power is Fire, his resource is Earth, and his self, friends, and competitors element is Metal.

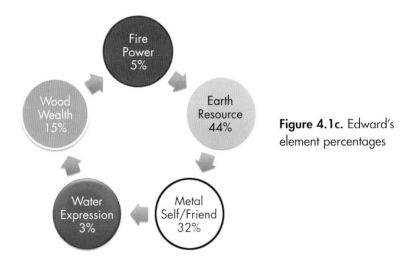

Figure 4.1c. Edward's element percentages

SELF, EXPRESSION, WEALTH, POWER, AND RESOURCE

Your Self

This element represents you and also describes your peers, friends, and competitors. It can denote your self-esteem and confidence and also ambitions and purpose. A lot of this element in your chart does not always mean a lively social life; a very strong personality with strong opinions can find it difficult to make and keep many friends. The nature of your friends will depend on how balanced your chart is, and whether your day master is strong or weak.

A weak day master—with little of this element—could be lonely if the element is very lacking but could also be more able to keep friends as the day master is less opinionated. A weak self can attract more help from friends than a strong self. If the same element as "self" is found in the other stems, then the friends are very visible; if they are in the lower part, the branches, then there is the suggestion of hidden friends, or hidden enemies or competitors.

The other phases must be compared in strength to your day master; the size of them in comparison to your self is the most important thing.

Expression

This is your child; you nourish and give birth to this element. It is your expression or manifestation, but all of that nurturing can weaken you if this element is much stronger than your self.

We can see this phase as an output in work, study, play, or artistic efforts, and when looking at our family as our actual children. It represents our intelligence and ability and can indicate motivation. Lacking expression in the birth chart can be the reason for shyness and an inability to assert oneself, but remember that Taoist astrology is dynamic. Each of the elements (all the phases of action) will come and mingle with our birth chart at different points in our lives, and our characteristics will fluctuate along with them.

The presence of this expression phase is a powerful antidote to the absence of other elements. When there is also a good wealth element, or wealth coming into the chart, then this expression element helps you to take advantage of the wealth being offered. It is your work, and without working you cannot hope to cash in on prosperity available in your wealth phase.

Wealth

The wealth phase is the element that your day master controls. In ancient Chinese life, this element was seen as the "wife" for a man; the thing he controlled but also the thing that made him rich. Although life is different today and women are often wage earners in a marriage, most men would still consider their wife to be a great asset for themselves and the necessary resource for family life. Today astrologers still interpret the wife as the wealth element of the man and the husband as the power element of the woman in a male-female marriage.

In astrology we generally interpret the traditional relationship to be a couple that is male-female. But not all people have it in their makeup to conform to this idea of romance or marriage. For both sexes it is real wealth and achievements; remember that money is considered to be just another energy in Taoist terms.

Count the number of times that your wealth element appears in your basic chart. Two to three times is good. More is not necessarily better, as too many appearances suggest that money is an issue for you. If wealth is totally missing it does not necessarily mean that you will be poor. The context of a life has to be examined too: wealth in a small village in a developing country would not be the same thing as wealth, or lack of it, in a Manhattan apartment building. Perhaps the wealth luck is not there in your birth chart but it will come in during the ten-year or annual luck cycles of your life. Be prepared to know how to earn it and keep it during those opportune periods.

If wealth is abundant, but only in the stems, it is visible in your life. You could be surrounded by wealth but not possess it; for example, as a bank manager or in a job that involved contact with great wealth which was not your own. If wealth is in the branches then it is more rooted and even hidden. If wealth is much bigger than your self then you could have problems taking advantage of wealth opportunities. Controlling your money and assets would be tiring; you might feel like it's "too much" or "beyond you."

The source of your wealth often corresponds to the element of your wealth.

> **Metal people**—Wood is their wealth. It will probably be associated with plants, growth, education, publishing, and so on; see the complete list of Wood characteristics and qualities in chapter 3.
>
> **Water people**—Fire is your wealth. Your money source is likely to be associated with fire, sunshine, electrics, performing, or explosives.
>
> **Wood people**—Earth is your wealth. Money can come from property, mining, land, farming. Earth is integral to all five elements and therefore Earth wealth can be associated with everything or anything.

Fire people—Metal is your wealth. Your money could come from planes, trains, cars, or weapons.

Earth people—Water is your wealth. This wealth could come from cleaning, cruises, boats, or the beverage industry.

Wealth is the relationship toward your grandchild; you control your grandchild, it is an indirect link, and it can be draining for you but is a source of satisfaction.

Power

Power is the element that has control over you. This can give you structure and self-discipline and can show how easy it is for you to be a good citizen and fit in with rules. However, too much of this element can be overpowering for your day master and could be interpreted that you are nonconformist and even rebellious or very rigid in concepts. For women this element is usually their ideal husband (see "Wealth," above).

When power comes into a woman's life during a luck period it indicates a likely episode for romance or meeting someone—the energy for the opportunity is there. Power is your grandparent inasmuch as it controls you, but controlling is tiring and you can wear this element out. A good amount of this element is essential to grasp the organizational skills necessary to achieve what you want or need to do. Too little or none can mean an inability to respect convention or rules; it can also mean that you are attracted to hierarchical organizations, which provide structure.

Resource

This is your parent element—it nourishes you. It is your family background; knowledge and thinking come from here. Too much of this element could make you a little lazy. Too little could leave you feeling that you need to do everything yourself, finding it difficult to feel that people are behind you helping and supporting you. Weak resource could also explain people who enjoy learning a lot, as they "feel the need" for more resources; the resource element is also an indication of education.

Remember from the description of the five elements that they are interdependent. If you have no expression then having a large wealth element will not make you wealthy. The expression phase between your self element and your wealth element ensures the flow of energy from you to your wealth. There is a parallel with the elements and your organs: having a weak heart and poor blood circulation would mean that the health of your other organs suffers even if they are strong.

All your element strengths are expressed on the chart as bubbles. You can also compare their strengths to your day master and to each other.

YOUR TEAMS

Looking at the five element circles and your five phases, now imagine two teams. One team is your money-making team or strengthening team: it is made up of your self (day master element) and the parent (resource element) that feeds you. The weakening team is your children, grandchildren, and grandparent phases (your expression, wealth, and power), which are effectively what you "spend" in life.

If your day master is weak look at your strengthening team. Is it your parent/resource element or your own element that is deficient? If it is your resource element that is weak, you will need to strengthen that during the practices; in turn this will nourish your self-element, strengthening you. If it is your self-phase that is weaker, then that is where you should concentrate your efforts.

As energy moves around in a generating cycle (Wood to Fire to Earth to Metal to Water to Wood), so you can move energy around your body during the Inner Alchemy Inner Smile meditations to the organs, as explained in chapter 5.

If you are a strong day master then you have a great amount of energy available that is "ready to roll." You can move this around your body during the Inner Smile meditation, which helps the other phases and their corresponding organs and takes the strain off your day master organs.

	HOUR	DAY	MONTH	YEAR
Stem	Yin Water	Yin Water	Yang Wood	Yang Earth
Branch	Buffalo	Boar	Rat	Horse
	Yin Earth	Yin Water	Yang Water	Yin Fire
	Yin Water	Yang Wood		Yin Earth
	Yin Metal			

Figure 4.2a. Conrad's birth chart

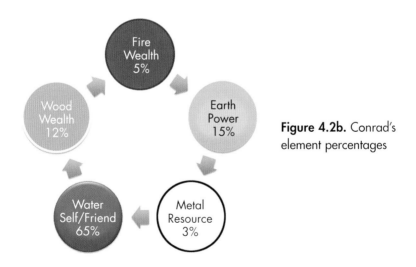

Figure 4.2b. Conrad's element percentages

Conrad is a very strong Water day master. We would expect an excellent communicator with a very quick, intelligent mind who is a self-made man. He would have some good structure to his arguments and lines of attacking a problem. However, his wealth element is so weak that unless he takes full advantage of additional wealth energy when it visits him he will not achieve the full potential suggested by his day master. With a strong, vibrant Water energy as a base for his Inner Smile meditation he can pull this energy around to feed the whole five-element cycle and revitalize his life and achievements. His expression should also be stronger to help the flow of energy, enabling wealth and marriage to be realized. He has a lot of friends and also a philosophical, self-questioning attitude to life.

From his birth chart data, we can see that most of those friends are ones who have the same polarity (yin or yang) as his day master. These friends will likely be good ones. He is Yin Water, and his other Water elements are all Yin Water bar one. He has a tiny bit of competition to keep him on his toes.

YIN AND YANG
AND THE TEN GODS

As we have discussed in chapter 3 there is a yin and yang of each element; the five elements show the yin and yang version as two different facets. One facet will be more "favorable" for the day master—you. This is based on the polarity of each individual's day master. Note that the polarity of the day master is in no way determined by the gender of the person; both men and women can be either yin or yang day master.

These ten facets (two for each of the five phases) are known as the "ten gods." The complete explanation of the ten gods is beyond the scope of this book, but the essential mechanics are given. You will be able to work them out for yourself using your birth chart in combination with the tables in this chapter, which also appear in appendix A for handy reference. Although "like repels like" and "opposites attract" are rules that can help to explain the harmony achieved when yin and yang fit together, note that this is not always the case for all of the five phases. The yin and yang elements we are talking about appear throughout your four pillars and also in daily, annual, and ten-year luck periods, which are explained in chapter 8.

Note Regarding Ten Gods Terms

The terms for the ten gods are translated from Chinese, and there are variations in their English equivalents according to the school of astrology, teaching master, or program. Mantak Chia has worked with programmers and astrologers to design two major astrology chart calculating programs for his website. See the table below. The terms in the middle column are the ones used by the older program (called *ziping*), which is also found on other sites. The terms on the left are the ones used in the more recent Inner Alchemy astrology program. Throughout this book we use the newer Inner Alchemy astrology program terms, but we have included this table of the equivalents for your reference.

TEN GODS EQUIVALENT TERMS

INNER ALCHEMY ASTROLOGY TERMS	ZIPING TERMS (OLDER TERMS)	CHINESE TERMS
Friendly Self	Friends, Self/Friends	比肩
Unfriendly Self	Competitive Self	劫财
Proper Expression	Proper Expression	食神
Opposing Expression	Powerful Expression	伤官
Proper Wealth	Primary Wealth	正财
Extra Wealth	Dynamic Wealth	偏财
Proper Power	Proper Power	正官
Hostile Power	Aggressive Power	七杀
Proper Resource	Primary Resource	正印
Hostile Resource	Inconsistent Resource	偏印

Let's take the example of a Yang Metal day master and analyze the other phases according to the day master's element and polarity. There are reference tables on pages 55–57 as well as in the appendix, where you can determine your own ten gods after the example.

For a Yang Metal Day Master

Self: Friendly Self or Unfriendly Self

Yang Metal—the same polarity as your day master—is considered "friendly self." Yin Metal—the opposite polarity to your day master—is friends and peers, but also competitors and rivals, "unfriendly self." Friends can also mean someone on your level of hierarchy in the family or your work structure.

Remember that competition can often spur you on, so it is not necessarily a bad thing. There might be a certain district of the town where there are many shoe shops, so people will specifically travel there to buy shoes; the competition is good for all the shoe shops. If one shoe shop was in a completely different part of town by itself, then perhaps not many shoppers would go there looking for shoes.

This competitiveness can range from friendly rivalry to envious backstabbing. It can sometimes be a case of describing you as having "the wrong sort of friends" around you. Where they appear in your chart is also significant. If they are in the stems, then they are quite visible in your life; if they are in the branches then they are not so obvious, even hidden, but probably connect deeper emotionally.

Expression:
Proper Expression and Opposing Expression

Yang Water is the "proper expression," inasmuch as it is output or production that comes from your natural talents and skills. The investments you make should give you the correct return. If it is your children, you raise them well and they become upright and independent as adults. They will help you when you are old. This is a good investment—proper expression.

Yin Water here is of a different quality and is known as "opposing expression." It is of a more aggressive nature. It can suggest a bad investment, like giving in to a child who always needs more and never stands on his own two feet or never treats you well when you are in your senior years.

Wealth:
Proper Wealth and Extra Wealth

Yin Wood is "proper wealth" and it is of a more constant nature than "extra wealth." It is sometimes equated with wealth earned as income from regular work, but not exclusively so. For a man, there will be more harmony with a proper wealth wife.

Yang Wood is extra wealth and it is more likely to be wealth from an unexpected win, an inheritance, or money that comes and goes. It is more easily spent but is not necessarily undeserved.

Power:
Proper Power and Hostile Power

Yin Fire is "proper power," and Yang Fire is "hostile power." Proper power is like parents telling you what to do because they love you—nagging, but in your own best interest. Some of this is necessary to structure your life well and fit in with society; it can also be seen as a higher government officer or teacher helping you.

As you can imagine, hostile power is not always in your own interest and can be harmful. It could be seen as a "bad policeman" or corrupt officer. The controlling element is also the attacking element, and certain controls are worse than others. Metal attacking Wood is very strong: imagine an axe attacking a tree. When Water attacks Fire it can extinguish it, another strong attack. The other "attacking" relationships could better be described as merely controlling and therefore less harmful: Earth controlling Water by soaking it up and curtailing its freedom, Fire controlling Metal by melting it, and Wood controlling Earth by absorbing it. Again the birth chart strengths are the determining factors. The nature of the effects can be sickness or danger.

Resource:
Proper Resource and Hostile Resource

Yin Earth is "proper resource," and Yang Earth is "hostile resource." Proper resource is the loving parental care and nurturing that feeds the day master. Enough proper resource ensures that the person is well prepared to do things.

Hostile resource is nurturing without the child's best interest at heart; it can be seen as a parent with poor parenting skills. A large quantity is "spoiling" to the day master, giving the child things he does not necessarily need. It can also mean not giving him the things he does need. In reality it can mean relationship problems with parents or a reluctant partner; it is an energy that can create general emotional turmoil.

More on the energies of the ten gods can be found in chapter 8.

FIND YOUR OWN TEN GODS

On the following pages are the tables listing the ten gods for each day master. Note that in these tables, the left column is the day master and the relationship expressed in the grid is the relationship that the element in the top line has with the day master. For example, in the first table (figure 4.3a, Yang Metal day master) when Yang Fire comes in it effectively attacks the day master, which is known as hostile power. The relationships between the day master and the other elements are different for each day master. As you can see in the Yang Wood day master table (figure 4.3e), Yang Metal is the hostile power of Yang Wood and would "attack" it. However, for Yang Metal day master (figure 4.3a), Yang Wood is extra wealth. Metal attacking Wood is the strongest "attack," but of course its strength to an individual would depend on the rest of the chart, the quality and the quantity of all of the five elements. In fact only by examining the strength of the day master together with the rest of the chart can we know exactly how detrimental or beneficial these phases are. In the following tables the "gods" in blue are the most desirable, those in red are the most challenging, and those in black are slightly challenging.

	+ Fire	+ Earth	+ Metal	+ Water	+ Wood
+ Metal	Hostile Power	Hostile Resource	Friendly Self	Proper Expression	Extra Wealth
	- Fire	- Earth	- Metal	-Water	- Wood
+ Metal	Proper Power	Proper Resource	Unfriendly Self	Opposing Expression	Proper Wealth

Figure 4.3a. Yang Metal day master

	+ Fire	+ Earth	+ Metal	+ Water	+ Wood
- Metal	Proper Power	Proper Resource	Unfriendly Self	Opposing Expression	Proper Wealth
	- Fire	- Earth	- Metal	-Water	- Wood
- Metal	Hostile Power	Hostile Resource	Friendly Self	Proper Expression	Extra Wealth

Figure 4.3b. Yin Metal day master. For a Yin Metal day master we can reverse the polarities in the table.

The next table, figure 4.3c, is for the Yang Water day master. Note that Yang Earth is a hostile power to Yang Water. However, what Yang Water does to Yang Fire day master is a stronger control: it extinguishes the flame (see figure 4.3g).

	+ Fire	+ Earth	+ Metal	+ Water	+ Wood
+ Water	Extra Wealth	Hostile Power	Hostile Resource	Friendly Self	Proper Expression
	- Fire	- Earth	- Metal	- Water	- Wood
+ Water	Proper Wealth	Proper Power	Proper Resource	Unfriendly Self	Opposing Expression

Figure 4.3c. Yang Water day master

	+ Fire	+ Earth	+ Metal	+ Water	+ Wood
- Water	Proper Wealth	Proper Power	Proper Resource	Unfriendly Self	Opposing Expression
	- Fire	- Earth	- Metal	-Water	- Wood
- Water	Extra Wealth	Hostile Power	Hostile Resource	Friendly Self	Proper Expression

Figure 4.3d. Yin Water day master

For both Yin and Yang Wood, Metal is a serious threat when its polarity indicates hostile power. It is like an axe to a tree. Its gravity always depends on the rest of the chart.

	+ Fire	+ Earth	+ Metal	+ Water	+ Wood
+ Wood	Proper Expression	Extra Wealth	Hostile Power	Hostile Resource	Friendly Self
	- Fire	**- Earth**	**- Metal**	**-Water**	**- Wood**
+ Wood	Opposing Expression	Proper Wealth	Proper Power	Proper Resource	Unfriendly Self

Figure 4.3e. Yang Wood day master

	+ Fire	+ Earth	+ Metal	+ Water	+ Wood
- Wood	Opposing Expression	Proper Wealth	Proper Power	Proper Resource	Unfriendly Self
	- Fire	**- Earth**	**- Metal**	**- Water**	**- Wood**
- Wood	Proper Expression	Extra Wealth	Hostile Power	Hostile Resource	Friendly Self

Figure 4.3f. Yin Wood day master

	+ Fire	+ Earth	+ Metal	+ Water	+ Wood
+ Fire	Friendly Self	Proper Expression	Extra Wealth	Hostile Power	Hostile Resource
	- Fire	**- Earth**	**- Metal**	**- Water**	**- Wood**
+ Fire	Unfriendly Self	Opposing Expression	Proper Wealth	Proper Power	Proper Resource

Figure 4.3g. Yang Fire day master

As an example, the following explains what we could understand by reading the Yin Fire day master table (figure 4.3h). Yin Fire is your chummy friend with similar energy, whereas Yang Fire is the competitive, envious one. Yin Earth brings you the correct investment; it is your proper expression. Yang Earth is the more doubtful opposing expression. You cannot always be sure of the nature of opposing expression. Yang Metal is your proper wealth; yin metal is your extra wealth. Yang Metal is the Mrs. Right—most compatible wife—element for a male Yin Fire day master and Yang Water would be the Prince Charming—most compatible husband—element for a female Yin Fire day master. Yang Water is also your proper power, Yin Water is your hostile power, and this particular Fire/Water relationship can be harmful.

	+ Fire	+ Earth	+ Metal	+ Water	+ Wood
- Fire	Unfriendly Self	Opposing Expression	Proper Wealth	Proper Power	Proper Resource
	- Fire	**- Earth**	**- Metal**	**- Water**	**- Wood**
- Fire	Friendly Self	Proper Expression	Extra Wealth	Hostile Power	Hostile Resource

Figure 4.3h. Yin Fire day master

	+ Fire	+ Earth	+ Metal	+ Water	+ Wood
+ Earth	Hostile Resource	Friendly Self	Proper Expression	Extra Wealth	Hostile Power
	- Fire	**- Earth**	**- Metal**	**- Water**	**- Wood**
+ Earth	Proper Resource	Unfriendly Self	Opposing Expression	Proper Wealth	Proper Power

Figure 4.3i. Yang Earth day master

	+ Fire	+ Earth	+ Metal	+ Water	+ Wood
- Earth	Proper Resource	Unfriendly Self	Opposing Expression	Proper Wealth	Proper Power
	- Fire	**- Earth**	**- Metal**	**- Water**	**- Wood**
- Earth	Hostile Resource	Friendly Self	Proper Expression	Extra Wealth	Hostile Power

Figure 4.3j. Yin Earth day master

TEN GODS ON
YOUR ASTROLOGICAL CHART

If you are using the full personal Inner Alchemy chart the ten gods phases will be expressed for you, otherwise you can determine them using the tables above in combination with your basic birth chart. Follow the example below (figure 4.4a). Notice how the ten gods information gives a more complete picture of the quality of the energies. Below, the quantities are expressed in the five-element bubble diagram and a pie chart of percentages. Later in the book you will see how this information can tell the story of this lady's life.

	HOUR	DAY	MONTH	YEAR
Stem	**Yang Earth** Hostile Resource	**Yang Metal** Day Master	**Yin Earth** Proper Resource	**Yin Metal** Unfriendly Self
Branch	**Tiger** **Yang Wood** Extra Wealth **Yang Fire** Hostile Power **Yang Earth** Hostile Resource	**Dog** **Yang Earth** Hostile Resource **Yin Metal** Unfriendly Self **Yin Fire** Proper Power	**Boar** **Yang Water** Proper Expression **Yang Wood** Extra Wealth	**Boar** **Yang Water** Proper Expression **Yang Wood** Extra Wealth

Figure 4.4a. Sample Yang Metal day master birth chart

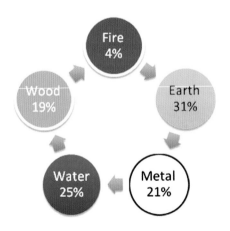

Figure 4.4b. Sample Yang Metal day master element percentages

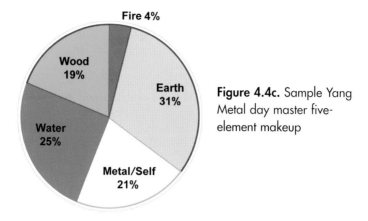

Figure 4.4c. Sample Yang Metal day master five-element makeup

FAMILY AND GROUP THERAPY

When studying the charts of a family with relationship problems—which could be most families to some degree—it is interesting to look at the relationships of their day masters. This applies also to a group of people at work or in a club, neighborhood association, or wherever people must interact together.

Before embarking on family counseling, it is worth examining these five-element relationships to explain why it might appear that a family member constantly "cuts" up another member. It also can explain why a parent has an apparent preference for one child, finds it easier to share a joke with another, or is more easily irritated by a third.

To use the following table (page 61) to study your self within a group or family, find your day master in the column on the left, then read off which elements represent the ten gods for you. The "gods" in italic print are the more desirable ones, while the ones in regular print represent energies that are more challenging for you. Together with the consideration of the ten gods, the relative strengths of the elements are the fundamental factors in defining the problems, harmonies, and lack of harmonies in our relationships.

Find the other members' day masters under the five columns to the right of the table to see what relationship this element is to you. Follow the top line as an example: if you are a Yin Fire day master you have a lot in common with other Yin and Yang Fire day masters in the office. But there could also be clashes and backstabbing with the Yang Fire ones. You might find yourself helping a Yin Earth fellow committee member more than a Yang Earth one. The Earth element is your child and Yin Earth represents better investment than Yang Earth. But they both might leave you unexplainably exhausted at times. You could feel very attached to your Yang Metal neighbor as you can control this element in a positive way; he should be very useful to you as this is your proper wealth element. The Yin Metal neighbor on the other side might not be as easy or satisfying to control; you might start behaving as his hostile power and wonder why you like to tell him what to do. If his day master is weaker than your own, then you will have the upper hand, which explains why he avoids you. As a weak Yin Fire day master, you would find a strong Yin Water day master to be overbearingly bossy. This is your power phase, so a stronger day master would want to put himself in a position of power around you. A weak Yang Water day master would be well meaning toward you in similar circumstances as the strength of day masters would be more evenly matched and this is "proper" power. But you have found a good parent in the Yang Wood day master in your yoga class—he will look out for you—whereas the Yin Wood one in the corner is going to leave you feeling upset over nothing.

To describe the relationships your family members have with each other, look at each member's day master on the left, then see how the other members of the group or family might affect him or her. There is a detailed example below the table.

You can also use this table to work out what incoming energies will mean to you when we look at the dynamic luck periods in chapter 8.

TABLE OF THE TEN DAY MASTERS AND THE ELEMENTS REPRESENTING THEIR TEN GODS

DAY MASTER	FIRE	EARTH	METAL	WATER	WOOD
-Fire	**Self** *Yin Friendly* Yang Unfriendly	**Expression** *Yin Proper* Yang Opposing	**Wealth** Yin Extra *Yang Proper*	**Power** Yin Hostile *Yang Proper*	**Resource** Yin Hostile *Yang Proper*
+Fire	**Self** Yin Unfriendly *Yang Friendly*	**Expression** Yin Opposing *Yang Proper*	**Wealth** *Yin Proper* Yang Extra	**Power** *Yin Proper* Yang Hostile	**Resource** *Yin Proper* Yang Hostile
-Earth	**Resource** Yin Hostile *Yang Proper*	**Self** *Yin Friendly* Yang Unfriendly	**Expression** *Yin Proper* Yang Opposing	**Wealth** Yin Extra *Yang Proper*	**Power** Yin Hostile *Yang Proper*
+Earth	**Resource** *Yin Proper* Yang Hostile	**Self** Yin Unfriendly *Yang Friendly*	**Expression** Yin Opposing *Yang Proper*	**Wealth** *Yin Proper* Yang Extra	**Power** *Yin Proper* Yang Hostile
-Metal	**Power** Yin Hostile *Yang Proper*	**Resource** Yin Hostile *Yang Proper*	**Self** *Yin Friendly* Yang Unfriendly	**Expression** *Yin Proper* Yang Opposing	**Wealth** Yin Extra *Yang Proper*
+Metal	**Power** *Yin Proper* Yang Hostile	**Resource** *Yin Proper* Yang Hostile	**Self** Yin Unfriendly *Yang Friendly*	**Expression** Yin Opposing *Yang Proper*	**Wealth** *Yin Proper* Yang Extra
-Water	**Wealth** Yin Extra *Yang Proper*	**Power** Yin Hostile *Yang Proper*	**Resource** Yin Hostile *Yang Proper*	**Self** *Yin Friendly* Yang Unfriendly	**Expression** *Yin Proper* Yang Opposing
+Water	**Wealth** *Yin Proper* Yang Extra	**Power** *Yin Proper* Yang Hostile	**Resource** *Yin Proper* Yang Hostile	**Self** Yin Unfriendly *Yang Friendly*	**Expression** Yin Opposing *Yang Proper*
-Wood	**Expression** *Yin Proper* Yang Opposing	**Wealth** Yin Extra *Yang Proper*	**Power** Yin Hostile *Yang Proper*	**Resource** Yin Hostile *Yang Proper*	**Self** *Yin Friendly* Yang Unfriendly
+Wood	**Expression** Yin Opposing *Yang Proper*	**Wealth** *Yin Proper* Yang Extra	**Power** *Yin Proper* Yang Hostile	**Resource** *Yin Proper* Yang Hostile	**Self** Yin Unfriendly *Yang Friendly*

Let us look at an example of a situation where a child is often considered a problem.

He is the youngest son, a Yang Fire day master. His father, a Yang

Water, is "harder" on him than on the other children. Yang Water represents the boy's hostile power. His elder sister is Yin Wood; she is his proper resource and is like a second mother to him. His grandmother is Yang Wood, his hostile resource, and is not as nice to him as she is to the other grandchildren. His mother is Yin Water, and she helps to keep him structured and organized. His elder brother is Yang Metal and finds him irritating; in fact the boy is hostile power to his elder brother who tries to avoid this. Luckily he has quite a few Yang Fire friends at school, although he often prefers to waste time with the Yin Fire ones. His girlfriend at school is Yin Metal, and they have been close since they met.

This is a simplistic example of how the energies interact. The ten gods will be explored again in relation to luck cycles in chapter 8.

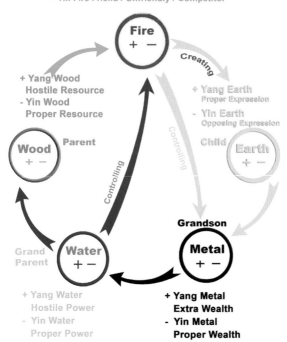

Figure 4.5. Yang Fire day master and the influences around him

5

Practices for Balancing Your Elements

Through studying the relative strengths of our five elements we can quickly determine which organs are most likely problematic and even which negative behaviors and emotions will dominate. Having a very strong element in the chart obviously means there are weak ones elsewhere, as seen in the following examples.

June has a very strong day master. Both the self element (Fire) and resource element (Wood) are strong, giving a total strengthening team that is much larger than her weakening team (explained in chapter 4 under the heading "Your Teams"). In figure 5.1b we remind you of the major organs associated with the five elements. In figure 5.1c we review the negative emotions stored in those organs.

The elements that are weak will need boosting to help the associated organs, and the elements with high energies have strong negative emotions. In this example the elements that need strengthening are the lungs and kidneys. The most important element to be balanced is her heart (Fire).

	HOUR	DAY	MONTH	YEAR
Stem	Yin Metal	Yang Fire	Yin Wood	Yin Fire
Branch	Rabbit Yin Wood	Dog Yang Earth Yin Metal Yin Fire	Snake Yang Fire Yang Earth Yang Metal	Boar Yang Water Yang Wood

Figure 5.1a. June's birth chart, a Yang Fire day master

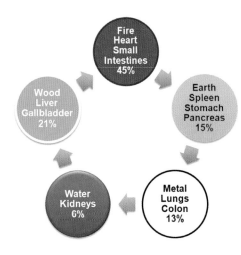

Figure 5.1b. Quantities of June's organ energy

Figure 5.1c. Negative emotions stored in the organs

Corrine is a very weak Yang Water day master. You can see that her weakening team adds up to much more than her strengthening team.

	HOUR	DAY	MONTH	YEAR
Stem	Yang Earth	Yang Water	Yin Fire	Yin Earth
Branch	Monkey Yang Metal Yang Earth Yang Water	Horse Yin Fire Yin Earth	Buffalo Yin Earth Yin Water Yin Metal	Ram Yin Earth Yin Fire Yin Wood

Figure 5.2a. Corrine's birth chart

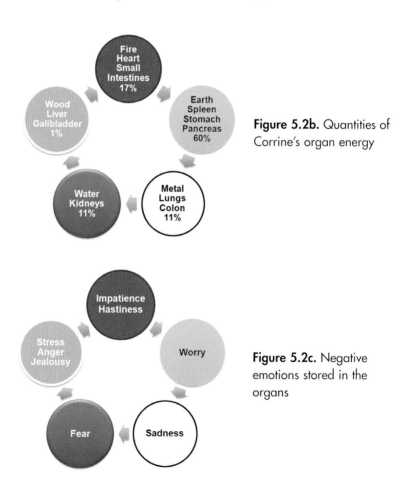

Figure 5.2b. Quantities of Corrine's organ energy

Figure 5.2c. Negative emotions stored in the organs

Corrine would worry a lot and be preoccupied with fairness. Such large Earth energy would mean that her Earth organs are vulnerable. Her liver energy is very low. Her day master organs—kidneys, bladder, and sexual organs—are also weak in energy and need more support than the other elements. Her Earth element would prove a heavy control for her day master; her Earth needs balancing. She is quite likely to have an Earth career as it is so dominating in her chart, and she would naturally put these enormous Earth talents and intelligence to good use.

From examining your own chart you will have already determined which of your elements need particular support. You are, of course, familiar with your own health concerns and will be able to see the relationship with your five-element makeup and those problems. If the weak element is your day master, you are more vulnerable in that element than if it is another phase element. However, weak elements in other phases do have an effect on the areas they influence. Let us look at the example of a weak Water element expression phase for a Metal day master—health implications might be kidney/gynecological problems; actively it might mean hesitant speech or an inability to work at times; emotionally it might mean fears or phobias. It is possible to have more than one weak element too, and they will all need attention.

We could also do the pentagon diagram for the sense organs, positive emotions, or other aspects to give you an idea of the relative strengths according to your five-element makeup.

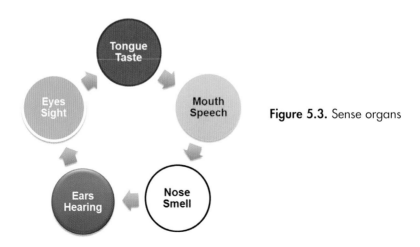

Figure 5.3. Sense organs

You will now be able to draw your conclusions about the negative emotions that are prevalent in you and the quality of the relationships and phases in your life.

SUPREME INNER ALCHEMY PRACTICES

The Supreme Inner Alchemy practices are the best way to work on emotional issues. They are powerful internal meditations that allow you to constantly treat and improve the physical body and emotional health. The "alchemy" is the change that will harmonize the five elements in you. That allows change in the physical organs and parts of the body controlled by those elements. It also allows changes in the nonphysical: the emotions and the action phases of your life.

In the above example of Corrine's weak Yang Water day master, we can conclude that she needs to strengthen her Metal, Water, and Wood elements. Strengthening Metal and Water gives her day master more support. On the physical level, it will protect her lungs and large intestines, and also her kidneys and bladder. Her Wood energy is very weak too, and it must be energized to protect her liver and gallbladder.

Using the Inner Smile meditation, and particularly the smile to the lungs, we are working on the negative emotions of grief and sadness. These emotions are immaterial essences, but balancing the Metal energy will improve physical health to the lungs. In this way we can go back and forth between the material, physical form and the immaterial, emotional essences.

The lung energy will then nurture Corrine's Water element that will in turn nurture her Wood element. Using the Inner Smile here she can move energy around the body. If we start the Inner Smile with the largest element—Earth in this case—then we have a lot of energy to move around the body through the generating cycle to finish in the Wood element, which is the weakest. Corrine can balance and diminish the vulnerability of her Earth element through the Healing Sounds.

During the practices, we can also use the Taoist rapid eye

movement technique to work on sad situations of the past, or fears and phobias. The exercise can delete these negative emotions. The Inner Smile is then used to return motivation and courage to the lungs and willpower to the kidneys. Heart fire, love, and happiness are all catalysts to the reaction. The physical state of the lungs and the other organs will improve through these exercises.

Western medicine has finally established the link between physical health and emotional problems, but this has been known to Taoists for five thousand years. When using the Supreme Inner Alchemy practices we are working on so many levels with many different connections. Refer to the table of elements, emotions, and organs (page 24). As the following image shows, this is not just a metaphor; the energy of the universe is physically present within the planets, our energy field (aura) and emotions, and our bones and organs. The universe's energies affect us every day, which is why it is so helpful to be able to keep all these elements in balance.

You have now had a good look at which qualities you have in your

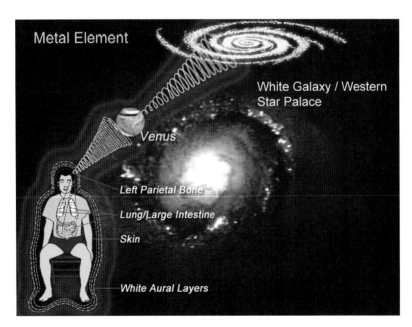

Figure 5.4. Metal element energy beams
down through Venus

elemental makeup. We imagine that you have also seen correlations between elements where you are imbalanced (weak or very strong) and recurring physical, emotional, and performance problems.

This book assumes that you are already familiar with Mantak Chia's Universal Healing Tao practices and are already either an instructor or a student. Therefore the following exercises are not described in a step-by-step fashion. We are talking about their specific application to your astrological chart information. If you do not know the practices well, we recommend that you look at some of the following material by Mantak Chia: *Emotional Wisdom, Transform Your Stress into Vitality, The Inner Smile, The Six Healing Sounds.*

Healing Sounds

The Healing Sounds meditation will bring balance to your chart. Start as usual with the lungs, unless one of the other elements is very strong. Start with the liver if there is a problem of stress.

In the example below of weak Yang Metal day master and weak Fire, the advice would be to start with the lung sound as taught classically and continue in the generating cycle (i.e., Water, Wood, Fire, Earth). For this type of weak Metal and weak Fire chart, if you have not got much time, concentrate on doing the lung (Metal) and the heart (Fire) sounds in the evening. If you can do all of the sounds three times, like the classical approach, do the Metal (lung) and Fire (heart) nine times each. Doing the Healing Sounds for the other elements that are already strong will not make them even stronger; the sounds harmonize and balance the organs. If you have a very strong element, which as explained earlier can be as problematic as having a weak element, then doing the sound for the organ concerned will help to balance it.

If an element is extremely weak, or even missing, do more of that sound. Throughout the day you can do the healing sound to the weakest organs subvocally, as often recommended for the stress cycle. Your own body and medical history will guide you when doing the Healing Sounds intermittently in this way.

In the case of a very weak element you can also work on other healing techniques, such as Chinese five-element nutrition (discussed in chapter 6) and Inner Alchemy feng shui (discussed in chapter 7).

	HOUR	DAY	MONTH	YEAR
Stem	Yang Water	Yang Metal	Yang Wood	Yang Water
Branch	Horse Yin Fire Yin Earth	Tiger Yang Wood Yang Fire Yang Earth	Dragon Yang Earth Yin Wood Yin Water	Dragon Yang Earth Yin Wood Yin Water

Figure 5.5a. Weak Yang Metal day master birth chart

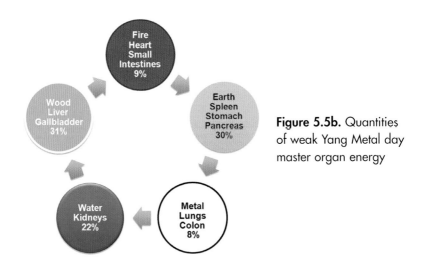

Figure 5.5b. Quantities of weak Yang Metal day master organ energy

Inner Smile

The Inner Smile meditation generates energy in your organs. It increases the positive emotions of the organs, leaving less space for the negative ones. If you have a weak day master and have suffered from the physical problems associated with that element, then the Inner Smile to that organ will reinforce it. This energy is real. You can feel it in your body during the meditation, and you can move it around using your mind and willpower.

If your day master or another element is very strong, start with that element so that you can spread that energy around the cycle. Having this very large energy already present means that you can take it to the other weaker organs, a bit like filling holes in a wall with a pre-prepared plaster mix. Always send heart fire to the organ to warm it before working on it. Otherwise start the Inner Smile with the heart.

This is an example of a normal day master and strong expression, but no wealth or power elements. This is for the birth chart, but remember that elements are constantly coming into your life in the form of luck period energies, as we shall see in chapter 8.

	HOUR	DAY	MONTH	YEAR
Stem	Yang Fire	Yin Fire	Yin Earth	Yang Earth
Branch	Horse Yin Fire Yin Earth	Ram Yin Earth Yin Fire Yin Wood	Ram Yin Earth Yin Fire Yin Wood	Tiger Yang Wood Yang Fire Yang Earth

Figure 5.6a. Birth chart with a strong expression element

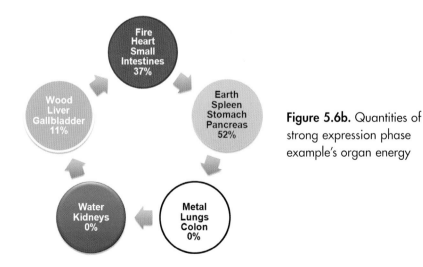

Figure 5.6b. Quantities of strong expression phase example's organ energy

We see that the strong expression phase, Earth, is much larger than the Fire day master. This is tiring for the day master; it is as if you are working relentlessly on something and you are spending more energy than you have. The Fire day master element itself is large, but together with the Wood resource element they are slightly weaker than the expression energy. This person would be a hard worker, intelligent, enjoy natural speaking skills, and be caring, charismatic, and always wanting to do things; however, he might not enjoy the wealth or achievements merited from his labors.

By starting the Inner Smile cycle with Earth and continuing through the usual generating cycle, you finish with Fire, the day master element. This will reinforce the day master, which needs help with this large amount of energy it is putting out. If it is not possible to spend a long time meditating it can help to do the punctual Inner Smile while taking a short break from work. In this example that would mean smiling to the liver, Wood, the resource phase, which will feed the self element, which would help store up for its continual expression work. Water and Metal are very weak—in fact not visible in the birth chart—and need some attention, too. The Healing Sounds would bring in much needed balance here.

The example in figure 5.7 below has an even larger expression

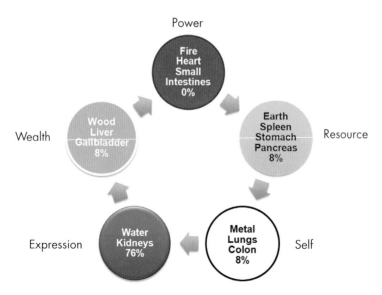

Figure 5.7. Weak Metal day master with very large expression

energy; this person cannot sit still for long. The activity is very draining for the day master. When Water is the expression phase it can
mean a lot of discussion, writing, and communication. However, as the
day master element is very weak the body is in more need of balance
than in the previous example. It would be very helpful to use the Inner
Smile to move that large Water energy around the body, finishing the
practice in the lungs. Even just smiling to the spleen (the resource
phase) would also help. However, only smiling to the lungs would help
to feed the already very high Water energy. Using the Healing Sound
for the lung in addition to the Inner Smile would be very harmonizing
and healing for the day master and the Healing Sound for the kidneys
would help balance the excessive Water energy.

Fusion Practices

Using the Fusion practices (found in *Fusion of the Five Elements*),
we can fuse all the negative energy together and use positive things

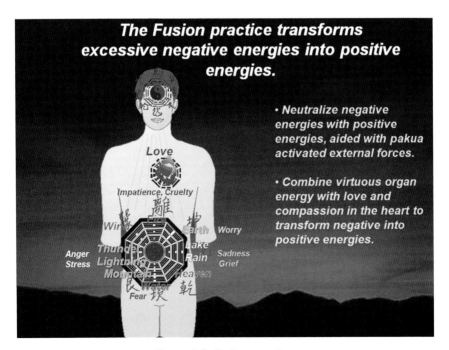

Figure 5.8. Fusion practices

Figure 5.9. Eight forces of nature expressed in the five elements
in the pakua position

to balance it out. In our modern life many people either confess their sins to God or to a psychologist, but in the Taoist way you can send them to the earth, composting them, and receive positive energies in return. It is a balancing process, and doing this you can really believe that you have the power to turn negative things into positive things. Using the pakua we are invoking the forces of nature to help us; the Fusion Meditations teach us how to print a pakua within ourselves.

6

Five-Element Nutrition, Aromatherapy, and Color Therapy

FIVE-ELEMENT NUTRITION

All foods are assigned an element, as they can both bring chi to the organs and lower the chi in an organ. The theory of five-element nutrition is based on the generating and controlling cycles. It is helpful to know which foods will affect your organs based on your astrological makeup.

Master Chia has spent over twenty years organizing and modifying his Taoist astrology program, which now includes five-element nutrition. During his years in the United States he researched many of the latest fad diets together with ethnic and medical diets. An important conclusion on diet is that there is no point in only adapting it to suit your body today; you must also look at the body you were born with as shown in your Taoist astrology chart.

The five-element nutrition section on the Universal Healing Tao website is a wonderful interactive tool that gives you information on changing your diet to balance your elements and improve your health.

Mechanics of Eating

Emotional issues affect the organs, and they also affect digestive juices. There is a lot of value to saying a form of "grace" before eating—starting with a thankful, peaceful frame of mind. For our modern busy city dwellers this could be translated into at least eating in a nice environment and taking a second to relax first. Food "on the go" is counterproductive; at least find a nice park bench if having a sandwich for lunch. Imagine the stress level of having to cross a busy street while eating a sandwich—perhaps your cell phone is ringing, too. A couple of minutes to relax and appreciate pleasant surroundings before starting should help set the scene. Find someone to say "bon appetit" to you.

"Chew your liquids and drink your food" is the Taoist saying that makes the point about the importance of chewing food well, thus introducing air, digestive juices, and chi into the mixture and so sending the food down into the stomach in a condition amenable to digestion. If this stage is hurried, then the stomach—which does not have teeth to break down food—cannot perform well and will send the mixture out into the intestines in an unacceptable condition. The intestines will not be able to absorb nutrients from it correctly: indigestion and/or constipation will be the result. The liver and other organs will thus be denied their full complement of nutrients, and imbalances due to your elemental makeup and possible emotional state will be exaggerated.

Emotions affect the quality of the saliva and digestive juices. Depression can turn the saliva bitter to the taste and increase the acid content. This in turn is bad for the digestion and the teeth as this acid in the mouth can eat away at the teeth starting with the enamel.

When a person is relaxed a hormone known to Taoists as "the longevity hormone" is released into the saliva. The saliva has a sweet and fragrant taste as a result. In addition to digestion saliva helps the body on many levels. It is nature's own moisturizer, aiding oral tissues, the digestive tract, and even facilitating speech.

Taoists refer to saliva as "the water of life," the "fountain of youth," and "Golden Elixir," to give you an idea of its importance. Saliva contains glucosamine, the amino sugar that is produced naturally in the body although its production depletes with age. Commercially produced glucosamine is one of the largest selling nonvitamin, non-mineral dietary supplements due to its role in cartilage regeneration. It is taken mainly by sufferers of arthritis, osteoarthritis, and painful joints, but also by athletes. Yet its natural production in the body can be stimulated by Chi Kung. It is released into the saliva, which has ten times more power to absorb chi than ordinary water. Saliva production too can be increased by very simple Chi Kung exercises and short self-massages. For more on this subject read or watch Mantak Chia's *Golden Elixir Chi Kung* and *Chi Self-Massage*.

Golden rules of Taoist nutrition include eating locally grown foods that are as fresh as possible and in season. That is the way to guarantee as much chi as possible in food so that it can then be absorbed by the body. Obviously choose organic where possible and avoid food produced using harmful products such as chemical fertilizers, pesticides on crops, or animal growth drugs. Read labels on prepared dishes even if the small print is challenging.

A Taoist expression advises treating your five organ groups like your five children: give them their five colors, smells, and tastes and you will be giving your body the necessary chi to fuel your five elements. Having noted what elements or organs need extra support for you, you can choose your meals by color or taste accordingly. See the table on page 24 for the five-element tastes and colors.

Food Chart

The Five Element Nutrition food chart on the website can be used in a couple of ways. Having determined which elements need bolstering you can click on the image of the organ and it will give you a comprehensive list of foods available around the world. You can also go to the "Five-Element Nutrition Alphabetic Food List" (www.tao-garden.com/5elements/Taoist5ElementsNutrition.ABC.html) to look at the components of a food. In both instances, the effects on the organ will be indicated. The list will note which foods are neutral, warm/ warming, or hot. These will bring more chi to your heart. The foods marked cold or cool will do the opposite. So if you have an excessively strong element in your chart you can calm down the excess energy in those organs by choosing to eat the cool and cold foods.

Each food is analyzed according to several criteria including acid/ alkaline, taste, and so forth. The five elements each relate to their own specific taste. Temperature is also an important factor on the list; all food stuffs are marked as cool, cold, neutral, warm/warming, or hot.

In our example of Cathy, a strong Earth day master with weak heart Fire, we see:

	HOUR	DAY	MONTH	YEAR
Stem	Yin Wood	Yin Earth	Yang Earth	Yin Earth
Branch	Boar Yang Water Yang Wood	Rooster Yin Metal	Dragon Yang Earth Yin Wood Yin Water	Ram Yin Earth Yin Fire Yin Wood

Figure 6.2a. Cathy's birth chart, a strong Yin Earth day master

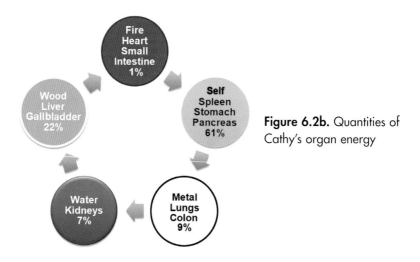

Figure 6.2b. Quantities of Cathy's organ energy

Cathy should calm down her strong Earth energy by choosing cool or neutral things on the Earth (spleen, pancreas, stomach) list, such as lentils and tofu. She should avoid stimulating the Earth energy with hot or warm foods like lamb and pheasant. To boost her low Fire energy she should choose hot or warm Fire (heart, small intestines) foods like ginger but avoid cold ones like wheat. She should similarly work on her Water and Metal chi by choosing warm or hot foods from those lists. Her liver energy is normal, but her liver organs could need support during different energy cycles in her life.

WORKS ON ELEMENT	FOODS AND HERBS	CLIMATE	ORGAN(S) Yin – Yang	
			Zang	Fu
Earth	Beans and Legumes, Lentil	Neutral	Spleen Pancreas	Stomach
Earth	Beans and Legumes, Tofu	Cool	Spleen Pancreas	Stomach
Earth	Lamb	Hot	Spleen	Stomach
Earth	Pheasant	Warm	Pancreas	
Fire	Ginger	Hot	Small Intestine	Heart
Fire	Wheat	Cold		Heart

Figure 6.3. Extract from the five-element nutrition chart

Another simple way to enhance your organ energy is to choose by color. To enhance liver energy choose green foods, such as green salad vegetables. Green is the corresponding color for Wood and therefore for the liver; those green vegetables are also very good for your body nutritionally.

To increase heart Fire choose cherries and red berries that are marked as "warming" in the chart, but go easy on white or yellow melon, as it is noted as "cool" for heart.

FIVE-ELEMENT AROMATHERAPY

At Tao Garden Mantak Chia has developed a five-element aromatherapy massage that involves using specially developed oils to enhance your weakest elements. The work in Tao Garden is adapted individually after consulting your astrology chart. The oils are concocted using herbs whose chi stimulates the elements. This special treatment results in an aromatherapy massage that is attuned to providing an enduring sense of well-being. The oils are available for home use.

INNER ALCHEMY COLOR THERAPY

The five elements all have their own colors. Supporting the element by wearing or sleeping in that color is the equivalent of raising its chi influence on you. Some feng shui cures involve adding or taking away colors from a decor for this reason, and of course the colors around you on your couch, bed, or walls will affect you. You have worked out which elements represent which phases for you and which ones you wish to enhance. Choose underwear or T-shirts when supporting an element through color: the closer it is to the body the more effective it will be.

ELEMENTS AND COLORS

ELEMENT	COLORS
Fire	Red, Purple
Earth	Yellow, Beige, Brown
Metal	White, Gold, Silver, Bronze
Water	Black, Dark Blue
Wood	Green, Light Blue, Turquoise

Although his day master Fire represents 21 percent, in Brian's chart it is considered weak. His strengthening elements are Fire and Wood. His weakening elements are Earth, Metal, and Water, which add up to more than his strengthening team.

To bolster himself he should wear red, which will also help his

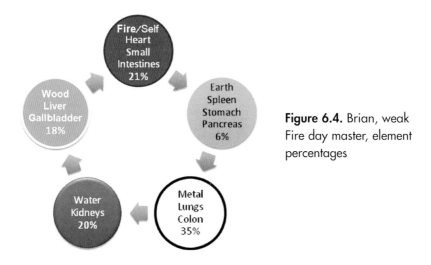

Figure 6.4. Brian, weak Fire day master, element percentages

expression and output as Fire feeds Earth. Green will also feed his person, as Wood is his resource phase. Dark blue or black could make him feel constricted, as Water is the phase that controls his day master and his Water is already nearly as strong as his self element. White adds to his already strong wealth phase, but his wealth phase is already much stronger than his day master. It is tiring for him to do this controlling, so that is counterproductive. Beige or yellow is Earth or his expression phase, so that could help him perform certain tasks at work, but it could weaken him because his self feeds Earth, and Earth feeds the already strong Metal.

Let us now look at the example of a strong day master: Conrad, a strong Water day master, whose chart is found in figures 4.2a and 4.2b on page 49.

Conrad's strengthening elements are Metal and Water. His weakening elements are Wood, Fire, and Earth. Therefore, he is a very strong Water person. A factor to the inner calculation is that he was born in a winter month, and an element is stronger in its own season.

Wearing dark blue or black strengthens an already very strong self. Green helps to drain the self and also is his output phase, helping him to get things done, feeding his wealth—which is quite weak—and enabling chi flow from his self to his wealth. Red bolsters up this weak

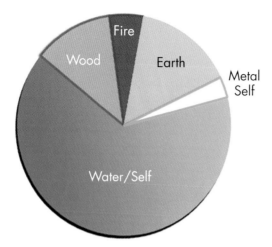

Figure 6.5. Conrad's element quantities, very strong Water day master

wealth phase and also helps drain off some of his self as it is tiring for an element to control; Water controls Fire. Beige or yellow means more control and self-discipline on his self, which is not a bad thing here as his self is so large. There is also the advantage of feeding his resource phase, which is very weak. Wearing white would bolster his resource phase but would in turn feed his day master, and it is already very strong.

So what colors would be most beneficial to Conrad? More than one in this case. Supporting Metal, his resource phase, indirectly by wearing beige is useful, as his Metal is so weak. Weak resource could give him the feeling of not having people or things behind him, whatever his circumstances. However, supporting the resource phase directly would feed his self element even more.

Green drains his very strong self directly, and indirectly feeds his wealth phase, which is weak. It also helps the flow of energy from his large, capable self through work (his output) into wealth to give him some results for his labor.

Inner Alchemy Feng Shui and Basic Chart Review

FENG SHUI, I CHING, AND THE PAKUAS

Feng shui is a very broad and complicated subject; understanding and practicing authentic Taoist feng shui with effective results involves many years of study and practice. It is neither mysticism nor superstition; there are fixed signs and real energies.

Feng shui masters hold a lot of knowledge in their brains and can calculate energies on their fingers. They will also have a good understanding of astrology and the I Ching (Book of Changes), which forms the backbone of the Five Taoist Arts (as Chinese metaphysics is often referred to). In feng shui the same principles of yin and yang and the five elements apply. Time is counted using the same heavenly stems and earthly branches as in astrology.

For the serious feng shui practitioner a complete audit on a home or business means also looking at the astrology of the person or persons concerned, as their compatibility with the space can be calculated as well as what prevailing heaven luck they have in their chart. Remember the interdependence of heaven, earth, and human luck in chapter 1; one side of this triangle cannot be completely ignored.

Effective feng shui auditing can be lengthy as both the time and the space of the building must be taken into consideration. In feng shui, "time" is the energy period of when the structure was built or greatly modified. "Space" is its location and direction calculated using compass readings of the building's front and its walls. The data must be accurate and the calculations used to define the building's energy are intricate. The surrounding energy created by mountains, roads, contours, and shapes must be added to the equation. After that, the interpretation requires much experience, and recommending changes equally needs skill and caution. It can also be confusing as there are several differing schools of feng shui methods.

Feng shui involves the use of the pakua, the eight trigram diagram of the universe and the seasons. The pakua is the result of the interplay between yin and yang, and displays the eight forces of nature—Fire, Earth, Rain, Heaven, Water, Mountains, Lightning, Wind—and the five elements or energies. The sixty-four hexagrams of the I Ching are paired combinations of two trigrams (eight trigrams multiplied by eight trigrams equals sixty-four possible combinations). The pakua is used in the Fusion of the Five Elements practices in the Universal Healing Tao. We have seen the pakua in chapter 1, figure 1.2 (page 7); and in chapter 5, figure 5.9 (page 74). Those images show the trigrams corresponding to each direction. The pakua below (figure 7.1) introduces the shapes and colors associated with the directions.

INNER ALCHEMY FENG SHUI

We live in a chi field and humans respond to chi.

Inner Alchemy feng shui involves using elementary feng shui tools to enhance your own elemental makeup according to the strengths and weaknesses you have now determined. It does not involve analyzing the energy chart of your home or building, other than using a simple compass to understand the directions. You do not need an

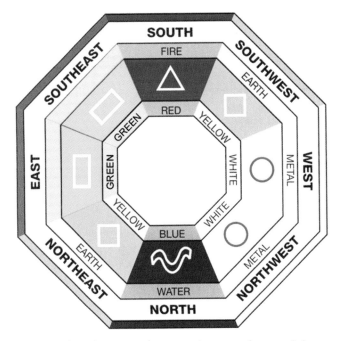

Figure 7.1. Pakua diagram: Elements, shapes, colors, and directions

expert to come to your home: you can do this for yourself after having studied your astrological chart.

As in chapter 5, the aim is to give support to an element, such as a weak day master, this time by strengthening that element in your home or immediate surroundings. The tools are the pakua, crystals, colors, and household and decorative objects in specific shapes and colors and other five-element methods.

This method is an external form of feng shui, as it is concerned with changing the chi in your surroundings, rather than within you. However, we are using force in the same way as in the Supreme Inner Alchemy practices. Where are the forces? We sit or we stand and the force comes down to us and affects us. Force from the north will affect your kidneys, from the east the liver, and from the south your heart. Force from the earth will affect the spleen and from the west it will affect the lungs. Refer again to the table on page 24. The universe affects the earth and all those upon it, no matter the distance.

Figure 7.2. Elements affecting our bodies and feng shui

Wherever we are, we are in the middle of all these forces; the pakua represents their ultimate combination. Inner Alchemy feng shui works by bringing the pakua inside of you to protect you. Using directions and simple colors we can apply this to our immediate surroundings for further support.

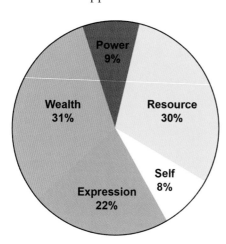

Figure 7.3. Weak Metal day master from figures 5.5a and 5.5b on page 70. The self element is Metal in white, the expression element is Water in blue, and so on according to the color scheme discussed in chapter 6.

For the above example, we would recommend putting a metal statue in the west part of her home or workplace. She could further support her Metal day master by wearing white, gold, and metallic colors, and sleeping in white sheets with gold color circle shapes. Other feng shui solutions for weak day masters are found in the list below.

>**Weak Water day masters**—Put dark blue or black objects in the north of the house; use a water decoration but not moving water. Use undulating line decorations and wear clothes with that pattern, also black and dark blue.
>
>**Weak Wood day masters**—Put a plant and/or something green in the east of the space. Wear green, turquoise, light blue, or sky blue.
>
>**Weak Fire day masters**—Put something red in the south of the space, and triangular forms, too. Wear something from the red-purple range of colors.
>
>**Weak Earth day masters**—Put stones, crystals, or rocks in the four corners and the center of the space. Wear yellows, beiges, browns. Sit near brown terracotta pots, pictures of sand, and deserts.

Please note that if you want to have moving water features in your home always observe the effects of energy, circumstances, and events for a week or so following their installation and activation. Do not hesitate to switch them off if negative events have happened. Moving water is a powerful feng shui tool and can have powerful effects on the energies of a space, but these can be negative as well as positive.

Your own personal observations linking events and energy to changes made to your living or working space are very important in feng shui.

Use the cardinal directions as indicated on page 88 for your feng shui supports and solutions.

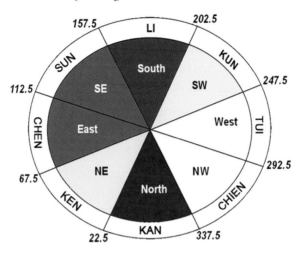

Figure 7.4. The compass divided into eight feng shui directions, including the cardinal directions

COSMIC FENG SHUI CLEANSING RITUAL

A building is fixed but we are alive and can move. We know how to take in force, how to direct forces, and how to move objects. There is so much energy buzzing around us every day: electromagnetic power, electric power, earth power. Just think of mobile phones, wi-fi, radio waves, and microwaves that we constantly turn on and beam around.

The earth has energy lines, ley lines, black lines, and underground water; one meridian of the earth cuts into another and that place feels different to us. Trees pick up these lines and grow "differently." You can sometimes feel these energies and you must pay attention to this feeling and work on increasing your sensitivity. We have already lost many senses that animals still have. Birds know when an eclipse is about to take place and groundhogs know when spring will come. Cats notoriously are attracted to negative energy places: they will find a black line in your house. However, if they are in your bed this is less significant as they also just like sleeping in your bed.

When you enter a building or room, what is your heart telling you? Do you feel good here? That butterfly feeling in your stomach—your second brain—can be telling you that something is wrong, that the energy is not good for you. Even if you use traditional feng shui but do not connect to the universal force, the old negative energies might remain.

So clear out negative energies in your house and in yourself. Call on the forces to clean out the energies around you.

Do this when moving in, when you feel a build-up of difficult energies blocking your progress or, like spring cleaning, when it feels right.

All of life is in the pakua and we want to have this pakua within us and enhance the forces. We can then use it for everything: to improve the feng shui in our home or in a temporary home, hotel room, classroom, meeting room. See *Taoist Cosmic Healing* and *Taoist Astral Healing* by Mantak Chia for these practices.

Sincerity is important, and to work with good energy you need to be sincere. Otherwise the chi is like a lovely dragon that has no eyes. No eyes means no spirit; you must be sincere. We believe that everything has souls and spirits. The organs are powered by universal force and they all have souls and spirits: the *shen* spirit (consciousness) in the heart, the *hun* soul (vision) in the liver, the *yi* spirit (intention) in the spleen, the *po* soul (body awareness) in the lungs, and the *zhi* spirit (willpower) in the kidneys. Treat the souls and spirits like babies; guide them in. If you have an awakening spirit, it cannot get there on its own. It needs assistance like a baby does.

In the West many believe we have souls and spirits and that God watches us mysteriously, like video surveillance. Taoists believe that house, local, land, and the direction spirits, or energies, all dwell in a house and in the area around it. Feng shui is about these energies. A traditional feng shui master will check around, look at these spirits, and put them in their right place. The house spirit, which is small and red and lies low on the floor, is the house ruler. The local spirit, which is equivalent to the mayor of the village or town, should be made to feel at home. There is also the land spirit, which governs a wider district or province around the house. For the earth spirit, one of the directional spirits, you can put rocks in the four corners and lay a gold leaf on them to activate wealth.

In Asia people traditionally invited in the spirits at the change of

Figure 7.5. Cosmic Healing Practice: the planets in connection
to the body during the house cleaning ritual

season or for the New Year when they cleaned out the house, including under the carpets and beds. But this tradition is somewhat lost
with the younger generation who work hard outside the home and
prefer to use their time off as leisure time. The direction spirits can
be honored in the following meditations.

MEDITATION RITUAL

To start: Facing the direction of north, invite in the earth spirit, local
spirit, and land spirits, then the great direction spirit of the North, the

blue spirit. Raise your hands up and receive the North Star (or we can use Mercury).

Feel blue light from Mercury or violet light from the North Star and let the forces come down to the north direction. Now turn counterclockwise to the west. With sincerity and gratitude connect your lungs with the white color and Venus power—the West spirit. Invite the white spirit to the west.

Turn to the south and connect your heart to the red light—the original spirit—and Mars. Invite the great spirit of the South and Mars to come down to the south: if you are sincere and grateful they will always be there.

Now turn to the east, connect your liver with the green light and Jupiter and invite in the great green spirit of the East. This is very powerful.

Turn again to the north, stand in the middle, and invite the great spirit of the Center. Connect your spleen to Saturn and the yellow light.

Command all five direction spirits to be present: the North, West, South, East, and Center spirits. Whether you believe in it or not, the energy is still there.

Learn the sequence and invite in the force in that order. Go to the north corner, although due north might not always be exactly in the corner. With arms extended in the air, ask for the force; when you feel the North force, clap three times or ring a Tibetan-style bell three times. That clears out the energy. State clearly "only allow good energy to stay here" and clap three times.

Repeat this for the west, the south, the east, and the center. This might make you think of Chinese New Year celebrations: setting off firecrackers around shops and homes as a way of clearing out old energy to welcome in new energy. Sometimes coffee, incense, or burning sage is used to clear out energy.

Use this ritual room by room, especially if you need to support an element within yourself. For example, if you need to reinforce the Metal in your elemental makeup, then do it to the west, invite in that energy. The energy will flow, so proceed to walk this energy around the room; the human body is the best conductor of chi. Continue with the other directions.

Ask and you will be given; let yourself feel the chi. If you don't feel it, you will not clean out the place. This ritual needs practice, so try it out and pause from time to time to see if you can feel the energy. Inhale it, then one, two, three, clap. Clapping a lot will help chase out the old energy, as will putting salt in the corners. Movement is yang energy, so the more that people walk around the room or come into the house, the more yang energy will be stimulated. A busy street of traffic outside your home or workplace is yang energy, too: roads are comparable to a flowing river in the ancient Chinese landscape where feng shui calculations were first mapped and crafted. Use this energy to your advantage. Yang energy stimulates activity, and job and money-making possibilities. Yin energy is stillness and quiet that is suitable for resting, health, and relationships. These principles are used in flying star feng shui.

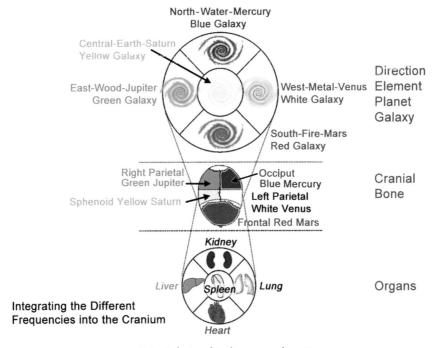

Figure 7.6. Relationship between directions, organs, colors, and galaxies

INNER ALCHEMY

It is easier and more beneficial to change the energy of a person rather than only changing the energy of his or her home, so please do the Inner Alchemy practices. The methods of Inner Alchemy feng shui attract energy and support the elements. Enhancing your earth luck will spur positive change in your human luck, which enables you to realize positive potential in your heaven luck. Do not just expect your house to look after you and provide you with the right chi you need for your prosperity, health, and relationships. Likewise if you have auspicious indications in your astrology chart (heaven luck), look on it as a potential that you can achieve through working with the elements. Work with sincerity toward your good intentions, remembering the interaction of heaven, earth, and human luck. Your sincerity and intentions can help transform the heaven and earth energies into something better for you.

SUMMARY OF
BASIC TAOIST ASTROLOGY

This book so far has given you many tools for creating and interpreting your birth chart, as well as suggested practices for balancing your elements and cultivating more harmony in your organs and emotions. You now have enough knowledge to make some positive changes in your self and relationships. Refer to the following list for a brief summary of the Inner Alchemy astrology steps, and remember you can refer to the tables in appendix A for easy access.

How to Create and
Read Your Birth Chart

1. Put birth data into the astrology chart program on the website, submit, and print out.

2. Identify your day master. (See chapter 3.)

   • Consider its strength: Is it strong or weak?

   • Look at the five-element relationship table on page 24 for information on your day master. Compare how you fare with the negative and positive emotions, organs, typical energies, and mental characteristics of your day master element.

   • Using the information on day master characteristics as a guide, ask yourself if you are using the positive talents and values of your stronger elements in your life and career. Could you be exploiting other element strengths for achievement and personal satisfaction? Does your day master need a lot of support?

3. Work out which of the Healing Sounds and other Supreme Inner Alchemy practices you should be doing to support or balance your day master.

4. Examine the strength and weakness of your other four elements as you did for your day master. Work out which of the Inner Alchemy practices can enhance and balance possible issues in the other four elements and integrate these practices with your chosen day master practices.

5. Determine and consider your ten gods (chapter 4).

   • Consider the polarity and relative strength of your self, expression, wealth, power, and resource elements.

   • Using the relationship table on page 24 notice the impact your strong/weak elements have on your life and health.

6. If you know the day masters of family or friends, find the ten gods they represent in your chart; this might hold some insight into your relationships.

7. Interpret your own feedback.

   • Particularly interesting is to record which elements you are trying to enhance and the practices you have undertaken to do so.

   • Note the effect you feel after following these practices for three or four weeks.

   • A bit of advice: Imagine that, as in bodybuilding, you concentrated on only one muscle and overdeveloped it in relationship to the rest of your muscular structure. This you would not do. Likewise you would not want to only work on one phase of your life (e.g. your wealth element) when doing the practices. Unlike bodybuilding, you would not be building that one element up to be out of proportion to the others. You would be neglecting the rest of your body, though, which does not align with the harmony and balance we wish to obtain. Remember that everything is interrelated.

8. Consider supporting weaknesses with other Taoist practices, such as five-element nutrition (chapter 6), color and aroma therapies, and Inner Alchemy feng shui (chapter 7).

9. Think again about the primordial trilogy of heaven, earth, and human luck. Can you see your decisions and actions (human luck) being influenced by your heaven luck (astrology) and earth luck (your environment and feng shui)? Can you relate the incoming energy phases to events in your life? Could working to harmonize all three lead to you exerting more control over your destiny by empowering your actions and decisions?

   This completes the basic information about your astrological self and the practices to create balance. If you are very interested in astrology, your next step would be to have a consultation with a Taoist astrologer. This would be extremely interesting, and now that you have learned some of the jargon and basics you would understand and appreciate it all the more. Mantak Chia's interpretations are very accurate and although he prefers to give only short readings that mainly look at health issues and how the practices can help you, he can refer to all aspects of your life. It is also interesting, to have your partner's chart (or the chart of someone with whom you work closely and spend a lot of time) read side by side with your own. The rest of this book offers some techniques to further explore this fascinating metaphysical science.

Luck Cycles

So far we have explored the energies that are present in your birth chart. However, there is another dynamic side of the story: the incoming luck cycles or periods. In this chapter we discuss these cycles and their effects on you. Remember you will need the more extensive version of your chart to obtain information about your luck cycles.

TEN-YEAR LUCK CYCLES

The ten-year luck cycle can be seen as a spotlight shining on a particular element or phase in your life. The luck period is expressed as a heavenly stem on top of an earthly branch, like the other four pillars. The heavenly chi from the top of the pillar is the chi that will affect the chart as soon as the luck period begins. The earthly chi's role will gradually become stronger throughout the ten years, being particularly effective during the final five years of the period. As we have mentioned before, the earthly influence is a more hidden chi—like a foundation—its elements are appropriately known as "roots." The heavenly chi is more visible and quicker to influence the person. Heaven energy is always faster and simpler than earth energy.

The program will calculate at what age the ten-year luck cycles start, as this is not the same for everyone. It is somewhere before the age of ten. Until then, the child is considered to be influenced by the luck cycle of his parents. Indeed the first luck pillar on a chart (reading from the left) will be the same as the month, or parents', pillar on the birth chart and will last from birth until the person's own ten-year-interval luck periods begin.

Whether the chart is for a man or for a woman, and whether the day master is a yang or yin element, determines the direction of the cycles that the heavenly stems and earthly branches take to form the ten-year luck pillar periods on the chart. As in the birth chart, the top line is the heavenly stem energy, and so on. The heavenly stem cycle goes either counterclockwise—the opposite direction of the generating cycle (Yin Metal, Yang Metal, Yin Earth, Yang Earth, Yin Fire, Yang Fire, Yin Wood, Yang Wood, Yin Water, Yang Water)—or clockwise in the generating direction (Yang Metal, Yin Metal, Yang Water, Yin Water, Yang Wood, Yin Wood, Yang Fire, Yin Fire, Yang Earth, Yin Earth). The direction of the cycle of the earthly animal branches can likewise go either clockwise (Dragon, Snake, Horse, Ram, etc.) or counter clockwise (Dragon, Rabbit, Tiger, Buffalo, etc.). The starting element is not the same for everyone; your starting element and direction of your cycle is calculated in the program and appears on your chart in the section titled "10 Years Luck Cycle." As each of these luck periods last ten years you would have to live to be a centenarian to have the heavenly stem element repeated, and of course very much longer to repeat the same stem and branch binomial.

The current ten-year luck cycle is like a "fifth pillar" whose relationship with the other four pillars must now be taken into consideration. The ten-year cycles explain why people's lives can take a big change in direction every ten or twenty years. These luck periods actually mean twenty years of each incoming element: ten years of the yin polarity and ten years of the yang polarity. From the chapter on the ten gods (chapter 4) we can see that the yang and yin elements have different influences on a person; one is usually significantly better than the other. However, they both relate to the same phase of the person's life and so will both affect that aspect. If the person's chart needs this incoming ten-year energy then life will be better; if it is not a desirable element for them then it can produce difficulties. The quantities and qualities of the elements in the original birth chart are what determine the effect of these incoming energies. Your chart will show which of the ten gods are visiting in any particular luck cycle.

TEN GODS REVISITED

Making interpretations and predictions based on luck cycles requires you to have a working knowledge of your ten gods. The more fortunate ones are self/friends, proper expression, proper wealth, proper power, and proper resource. The less fortunate ones are unfriendly self/friends/competitors, opposing expression, extra wealth, hostile power, and inconsistent resource. Of the less fortunate energies the worse by far are hostile power and hostile resource. This summary can only be a generalization and the real picture is completely dependent on the quantities in your basic birth chart. The area of your life where you would have these problems is indicated by its position in your chart (more on this in chapter 10). So be prepared for the good luck coming your way, or the opposite.

Here is an overview of what these incoming energies might mean for you:

> **Hostile Power:** If your hostile power is present it can mean attacks on all fronts. This could be in terms of accidents, sickness, mishaps, or danger.
>
> **Proper Power:** Coming into your life this is generally positive, indicating an improvement in personal structure and organization and possible hierarchical rise. For a woman this can also indicate the appearance of a love interest, like being sprinkled with fairy dust.
>
> **Hostile Resource:** This can be serious, and negative effects are generally manifested as relationship problems or emotional turmoil.
>
> **Proper Resource:** This gives you good backing or an increase in support and will strengthen your day master.

Proper Wealth: This indicates money coming from an earned source, the fruits of your work. If you can see more than one wealth element heading your way, be prepared to take advantage of it. It does not mean money literally dropping from heaven. Whether you can achieve the wealth available depends on how strong your self and your expression phases are.

Extra Wealth: Is just that . . . wealth coming from an unexpected source such as an inheritance or a big win. It is rarely considered unfortunate to receive the extra wealth even though it is the "wrong" polarity of the element. Remember that wealth can also mean love interest for a man, but in that case extra wealth may not be as appropriate as primary wealth.

Friendly Self: Seeing your friendly self element means support for you. However, if your day master is very strong, it might not be a good thing for your self to be strengthened. You might no longer be able to listen to others.

Unfriendly Self: This may mean some backstabbing from someone at work or around you; it could also mean friends who distract you from what is good for you.

Proper Expression: This will be good news for you unless your expression is already much bigger than yourself; in that case it will be tiring. Expression also represents your investments; proper expression is a good investment for you, good working energies.

Opposing Expression: This could be a bad investment, not doing your work well, or choosing a wrong path in work or study, and it is very poor investment energy. It means quite simply that you will not get a return on an investment made.

Let us look at how this energy will affect a person.

	HOUR	DAY	MONTH	YEAR
Stem	Yin Metal	Yang Water	Yin Fire	Yang Metal
Branch	Buffalo	Tiger	Boar	Horse
	Yin Earth	Yang Wood	Yang Water	Yin Fire
	Yin Water	Yang Fire	Yang Wood	Yin Earth
	Yin Metal	Yang Earth		

Figure 8.1a. Jay's birth chart, strong Yang Water day master

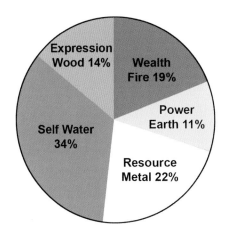

Figure 8.1b. Jay's element percentages

	0–1 YEAR	1–10 YEARS	11–20 YEARS
Stem	**Yin Fire**	**Yang Earth**	**Yin Earth**
	Proper Wealth	Hostile Power	Proper Power
Branch	**Boar**	**Rat**	**Buffalo**
	Yang Water	**Yin Water**	**Yin Earth**
	Friendly Self	Unfriendly Self	Proper Power
	Yang Wood		**Yin Water**
	Proper Expression		Unfriendly Self
			Yin Metal
			Proper Resource

Figure 8.1c. Extract from Jay's ten-year luck cycles

For this example we have taken an extract of the beginning of the cycle. Jay's first ten-year luck cycle started at the age of one and, as he is a yang male, the stems on the top line go in the generating cycle of the elements. So the ten-year luck cycles following figure 8.1c will continue: Yang Metal, Yin Metal, and so forth, on the heavenly stem line. As Earth energy is always more complicated, the ten-year cycle would continue with Yang Water, Yin Water, Yin Earth, Yang Wood, Yin Wood, Yang Earth, Yang Fire, Yin Fire, Yin Earth, Yang Metal, Yin Metal, Yang Earth, Yin Water. This is the order of the animals. For a yin day master, this order of the branches is reversed.

From figures 8.1a and b, we can see that Jay is a strong Yang Water person. In figure 8.1c, we can see that his own first ten-year luck period began at the age of one and that hostile power (heaven's energy as it is in the top line) from age one would have given him a variety of problems, usually health related.

From the age of eleven he would have found a lot more structure in his life as it is now Yin Earth, proper power, which is coming down from heaven; this could well have been seen as things going well in his school life. The earthly energy from the bottom line gradually increases its strength, so approximately half way through his second cycle—at age fifteen—he would have seen an increase in friends, but not always the right ones. These energies together might well have been lived as "trouble at school." However, there would be an increase in the beneficial structure from the Earth energies increasing intensity at around the age of sixteen. The Earth energy from his natal chart is not enough to keep his strong self element—Water—under control and performing efficiently. A strong Water day master is an intelligent, thoughtful person and this new energy phase could show up as realizing great potential academically, but from his birth chart we can see that he will struggle with the influences of positive and negative friendships.

Proper resource is also coming to Jay, so that should hopefully include the judgment necessary to deal with these issues. This good resource can manifest itself in many ways. On the human level it could be closeness to parents—particularly the mother—or mentors; it can also represent an awakening of knowledge and responsibility within himself and self-confidence. Resource is something that is continually nurturing you; having good resource means that you have ingested that "food for life." So having good resource makes it fairly easy to get going on something, provided that there are the day master and expression phases to do it. Resource also ensures a good chi flow from the power element, which helps self-organization, to the day master.

Difficulties can help forge positive characteristics in a person and the adversity of the hostile power suffered in Jay's early childhood could well help him in later life. The way people deal with adversity of course depends on the diverse energies present at birth, and also by the circumstances and people around them. Ultimately the decisions a person makes become a part of the picture. This brings us back to the human in the three treasures: heaven, earth, and human luck. The earth luck dictates to a certain degree if the person is in the right place and environment to benefit from favorable energies coming into his or her chart.

In the case of our example above (see figure 8.1c), Earth comes in from the ages of one to twenty. This is the weakest element in his birth chart and so will help this phase of his life. It will help to give him more structure and organization skills during those early years when they are otherwise weak in him.

It is very interesting to read the charts of elderly people and to see how the incoming luck periods have affected them. It is important to mention that charts generated by computer programs do not predict when life will end. In most programs the charts have as many luck periods as will fit the size of the paper rather than the actual number the person will live through (which cannot be predicted using this method). We will now consider the ten-year luck cycles' effects on an older person.

The pie chart shows that there is no Metal in her birth chart. However, Metal would have come in during her lifetime, so we would not expect someone who is totally without wealth—remember that wealth can also be other achievements. Physically she could have suffered from weak lungs or large intestine but her heart and other organs are strong.

	HOUR	DAY	MONTH	YEAR
Stem	**Yang Wood** Hostile Resource	**Yang Fire**	**Yang Fire** Friends	**Yin Water** Proper Power
Branch	**Horse** **Yin Fire** Unfriendly Self **Yin Earth** Opposing Expression	**Dragon** **Yang Earth** Proper Expression **Yin Wood** Proper Resource **Yin Water** Proper Power	**Dragon** **Yang Earth** Proper Expression **Yin Wood** Proper Resource **Yin Water** Proper Power	**Boar** **Yang Water** Hostile Power **Yang Wood** Hostile Resource

Figure 8.2a. Joy's birth chart normal strength Yang Fire day master in her eighties

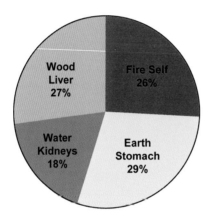

Figure 8.2b. Joy's element percentages

	77–86 YEARS	87–96 YEARS
Stem	**Yang Wood** Hostile Resource	**Yin Wood** Proper Resource
Branch	**Rat** **Yin Water** Proper Power	**Buffalo** **Yin Earth** Opposing Expression **Yin Water** Proper Power **Yin Metal** Proper Wealth

Figure 8.2c. Two of Joy's ten-year luck cycles

Looking at figure 8.2c and comparing these two decades in Joy's life we can see that there are better energies coming in at eighty-seven years old than in the preceding ten years. In the preceding decade, the hostile resource—Wood—would have brought emotional difficulties to her life plus health problems attacking the stomach, spleen, and pancreas. But the proper power will have contributed to good order in her life as the Water energies increased in strength around eighty-two years of age. When the proper resource arrives at eighty-seven years of age it will support her day master and her heart, and therefore all of her body. Although already a fine age, she could have some improvements in overall health and quality of life at that point.

ANNUAL LUCK

Each year of those ten-year luck periods will also have the annual year's energy to be taken into consideration. The annual luck period is easier to calculate as it is the same for everybody. It is simply the stem and branch of the Chinese year—for example, the Yang Metal Tiger year starts February 4, 2010, and goes until February 4, 2011 (see table on pages 11–13). The heavenly stem is Yang Metal and the earthly branch is Tiger. Tiger energies are predominantly Yang Wood with some smaller hidden Yang Fire and Yang Earth. Although many astrology columns will give predictions for what will happen to us all from reading the animal of the year (Tiger for 2010, Rabbit for 2011, etc.), it is the heavenly stem influence that is stronger and quicker to make its energies felt. Of course how these five elements and ten gods affect us will depend on our birth chart (see ten gods tables, figures 4.4a–4.4j).

We will now look at how adding on the annual luck elements to the original four pillar chart plus the current ten-year luck cycle might influence a life.

	HOUR	DAY	MONTH	YEAR
Stem	Yang Earth	Yang Water	Yin Fire	Yin Earth
Branch	Monkey Yang Metal Yang Earth Yang Water	Horse Yin Fire Yin Earth	Buffalo Yin Earth Yin Water Yin Metal	Ram Yin Earth Yin Fire Yin Wood

Figure 8.3a. Constance's birth chart, weak Yang Water day master

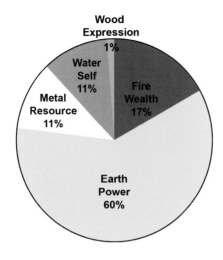

Figure 8.3b. Constance's element percentages

| | 2009–2018 | 2019–2028 |
	29 YEARS–38 YEARS OLD	39–48 YEARS OLD
Stem	**Yang Metal** Hostile Resource	**Yin Metal** Proper Resource
Branch	**Dragon** **Yang Earth** Hostile Power **Yin Wood** Opposing Expression **Yin Water** Unfriendly Self	**Snake** **Yang Fire** Extra Wealth **Yang Earth** Hostile Power **Yang Metal** Hostile Resource

Figure 8.3c. Two of Constance's ten-year luck cycles

	2010	2011
Stem	**Yang Metal** Hostile Resource	**Yin Metal** Proper Resource
Branch	**Tiger** **Yang Wood** Proper Expression **Yang Fire** Extra Wealth **Yang Earth** Hostile Power	**Rabbit** **Yin Wood** Opposing Expression

Figure 8.3d. Constance's annual luck for two years

Look at how the annual luck calculation will add more information to Constance's chart. As Constance is in her 29–38 year cycle, she will have already experienced some emotional upsets or relationship problems from the hostile resource energy. The decade following is the proper resource phase, which will promise fewer relationship problems. Taking into account the annual luck we could pinpoint some difficult events in 2010, as again we have hostile resource coming in. However, 2011 gives her proper resource within the ten-year hostile resource phase, so there is the chance of having better relationships. Remember that this is a prediction of possibilities based on astrology showing prevailing energies, but it is not fortune telling or clairvoyance. Constance has such a strong Earth element that she can move some of that energy around to Metal (her resource) and then to Water (her self element) using the Inner Smile meditation.

Having such a strong element in your birth chart gives you a significant opportunity to move energy around for the better. This strong Earth is Constance's power phase; she is very well-organized, sensitive, and caring. It indicates great talents and capacities for work in real estate, building, teaching, the caring professions, and managing people or companies. It also indicates being at ease with great responsibilities or power.

LUCK CALCULATION

Every minute, hour, day, and month has an energy, and this too can be calculated. There are feng shui methods that calculate the best time to take action based on this. For yourself, you might remember that the ten elements turn in a continual cycle, and so that if this year is a Yang Metal year, then next year is a Yin Metal year, the year after will be a Yang Water year, and so on.

The heavenly stem is much more significant than the earthly branch in the year and day energy. You need to pay less attention to the animal branch and the sixty-year binomial cycle. Just follow the ten gods cycle and observe their impact on you and your life.

As we look at the years to come, that is where the traditional prediction aspect of astrology comes in. A prediction will show the possibility of positive or negative things happening in aspects of your life according to the phase of the incoming energies (self, expression, wealth, power, and resource). Astrology can even show you where in your life these events might happen. For example, if it is in your marriage palace (see chapter 10), then that is where the change in energy will occur. Looking back over your past you might be able to see that a relationship that seemed suitable could have failed because the energy was not there to support it. Likewise in your career or education, perhaps the energy at certain critical times was not in your favor. When the right energy is there in the future, you should be able to recognize it and take advantage of it.

Energy is calculated in a sixty-year or sixty-day cycle. To calculate daily luck it is enough to just see which of the ten basic heavenly energies are coming in that day, and whether it is the yin or yang of the five elements. This information would be available in a Chinese almanac, and our own Inner Alchemy astrology web page gives hourly, daily, monthly, and annual calculations for the moment you connect with it. This is a very good daily energy guide.

Having calculated your day master and what phases correspond to the other four elements in your chart, and having looked at the ten gods chapter, you can now plan with those energies. Make observations about yourself, your chart, an activity that you are trying to achieve, and what happens during each day of a ten-day cycle. From there you can choose the most fortunate element day to act on projects, work, make hospital appointments, major purchases, or marriage proposals. Likewise you can choose a day to capture the best energies for Chi Kung to enhance the heart, spleen, lungs, kidneys, or liver. Many Chi Kung practices are performed according to the season—liver work in the spring, kidney work in the winter—in order to use seasonal energies at their best.

If you have work to do, decisions to make, contracts to sign, and so on, using the right day is adding an element of luck and also avoiding a day with more challenging energies to do that task. There are date and time selection methods that are used professionally to launch projects, but the complexities of working with hour energy is not generally worth it. Spending too much time on calculating a time takes away that precious time you could use to do your Chi Kung and meditation practices. Always remember the trilogy of heaven, earth, and human energies. If you are not putting intention in the form of meditation or Chi Kung into the day or year energy, then something big is missing. Do not expect to simply calculate the day's energy and let heaven do it all for you.

Combining your good intentions and your attention with heaven's energy will bring you more chance of success.

Figure 8.4 covers a ten-day cycle of daily luck for the dates of the Tao Congress "Pearls of Wisdom" in September 2010 at Tao Garden.

SEPT. 2010	5	6	7	8	9	10	11	12	13	14
Stem	Yang Earth	Yin Earth	Yang Metal	Yin Metal	Yang Water	Yin Water	Yang Wood	Yin Wood	Yang Fire	Yin Fire
Branch	Horse	Ram	Monkey	Rooster	Dog	Boar	Rat	Buffalo	Tiger	Rabbit

Figure 8.4. Sample ten-day luck cycle

As the heavenly stem is so much more powerful in the daily luck pillar we have given only the name of the animal in the branch line, but you can refer to the table on page 113 for the branch energies if you would like to know them.

You can further increase the power of your practices by being aware of which daily energy is available. If you wish to increase your Wood element, be aware of the extra liver energy available while meditating on Wood days—September 11 and 12 in the table above. Smile to your liver and breathe in the green light from the green galaxy, stocking your liver with kindness and generosity; push out frustration, stress, envy, and anger.

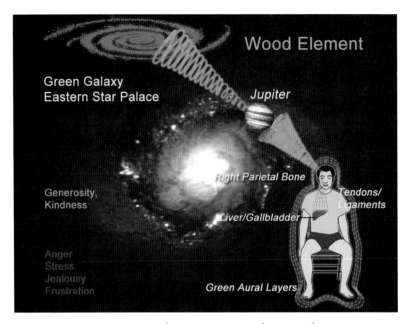

Figure 8.5. Meditating on a Wood energy day

At the end of the next chapter we will look at special conditions and cases that influence the luck cycles.

9

Animals, Clashes, and Trinities

CHINESE ANIMALS— THE EARTHLY BRANCHES

We have learned that Chinese astrology is much more than the popularized "what animal are you?" variety. All of the branches in your birth chart are expressed in animals, but it is the year branch animal that defines "what animal you are."

The energy of a time period can share characteristics with the animal it is named after. Most Chinese astrology books will describe your animal and suggest that is "you." You might well find some aspects of your animal in you, but keep in mind that there are many components to your astrological makeup—including your day master, which is not expressed as an earthly branch animal but instead comes from the heavenly stems.

We can divide the animals roughly into four groups:

> **The Competitors**—The Rat, Monkey, and Dragon are active, positive, competitive, and determined individuals. The Dragon is courageous, enthusiastic, and self-confident; the Rat is intelligent and quick to see an

opportunity, but insecure; and the Monkey is as crafty as his stereotype suggests.

The Independents—The Horse, Dog, and Tiger are the emotional, free-spirited, highly principled, liberty-loving animals. The Horse is emotional and good at strategy, but restless. The Tiger is ferocious, strong, and impulsive; and the Dog is calm, good-natured, and determined to finish projects.

The Intellectuals—The Snake, Rooster, and Buffalo. The Buffalo is stable and well grounded. The Snake is charming and diplomatic, but cunning and ambitious. The Rooster is flamboyant and does not mince his words. They are the visionary thinkers.

The Diplomats—The Rabbit, Ram, and Boar. The Rabbit is quick to analyze and good at strategy. The Ram is very generous and gentle. The Boar is strong. None of them are risk takers or very cunning. They do not enjoy a high profile but are good at mutual support.

In the sixty-year cycle of time each animal appears five times; they are matched with each of the five elements when combined with the heavenly stems (see table on pages 11–13). So if you are a Rat, for example, you could be a Wood, Fire, Earth, Metal, or Water Rat. There is a subtle difference in the energies of these five Rats. If you are a Wood Rat born in 1924, then it would be 1984 before you found yourself back in the Wood Rat year. It takes the full sixty years for the cycle to get back to the same year energy that you were born in.

All of the animals have a main element and a polarity. Some of the animals also have one or two minor elements, or hidden roots (see table on page 113).

THE BRANCHES AND THEIR ELEMENTS

BRANCH	MAIN ELEMENT	HIDDEN ROOTS
Rat	Yin Water	
Buffalo	Yin Earth	Yin Water, Yin Metal
Tiger	Yang Wood	Yang Fire, Yang Earth
Rabbit	Yin Wood	
Dragon	Yang Earth	Yin Wood, Yin Water
Snake	Yang Fire	Yang Earth, Yang Metal
Horse	Yin Fire	Yin Earth
Ram	Yin Earth	Yin Fire, Yin Wood
Monkey	Yang Metal	Yang Water, Yang Earth
Rooster	Yin Metal	
Dog	Yang Earth	Yin Metal, Yin Fire
Boar	Yang Water	Yang Wood

Yearly Predictions Based on Your Animal

Predictions for the year usually remain very general and are based on the effects of the incoming animal energies onto your yearly animal energies, which are shown in your birth chart. But the effects of the year energies will not be the same for everybody; only by looking at your entire chart can we understand what the year's energy will mean to your day master and the balance of the five elements that you were born with. As you see in the table above, Rat, for example, is Yin Water, so there are basic predictions that can be made suggesting how the "energy" of a particular year would be for the Rat—and of course the other eleven animals.

Predictions for Rat: 2010–2012

Let's continue with Rat as an example, through the years 2010 to 2012. The year 2010 was a Yang Metal Tiger year; Yang Metal is the heavenly energy. These energies will have an immediate effect on our Rat. The Earth energy for the year is Tiger, which is made up of Yang Wood with some Yang Fire and Yang Earth hidden roots (see table above). This stem energy, Yang Metal, is the proper resource phase for Rat (see table on page 61 for a reminder of how the phases correspond with the day master); however, if we are only looking at 2010's year animal, Tiger, we would note that the Tiger's Yang Wood represents expression for the Rat. The Rat would be weakened by the Wood energies present in the year branch for 2010. In fact, as we have seen in chapter 4 on the ten gods, Yang Wood represents opposing expression for Rat's Yin Water day master.

The year 2011 is Yin Metal Rabbit; Rabbit is Yin Wood. The heavenly energy, Yin Metal, for this year is resource again, but unlike 2010, this year it is hostile resource for the Yin Water in Rat. The Yin Wood branch energy is still expression, but this time proper expression.

The year 2012 is Yang Water Dragon; Dragon is Yang Earth, with Yin Wood and Yin Water hidden roots. For Rat's Yin Water the good friend (or friendly self), hidden root Yin Water, comes in at the end of the year, but some competitive energies (or unfriendly self)—Yang Water—come in at the beginning of the year with the Yang Water heavenly stem part of the annual luck pillar. Predictions of yearly events for 2012 for the planet as a whole are based on the image of Yang Water on top of Yang Earth (Dragon), as in tidal waves or earth shifting.

Animal Compatibility

We can read our animal sign and that gives us some insight into behavior and why we get on better with some people. But it is different from our day master and does not provide us with the intricate and deeply meaningful interpretations possible when working from the day master. When the animals are pictured in the cycles of the seasons, we can see the relationships between them more easily. There

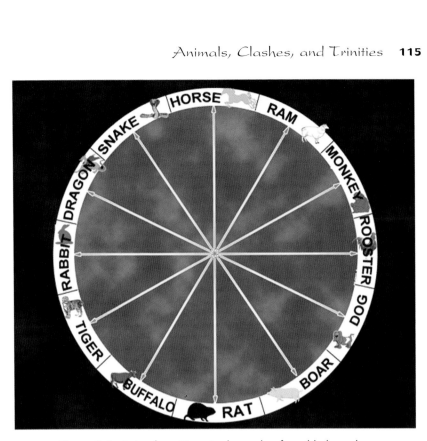

Figure 9.1. Animal positions in the cycle of earthly branches

are alliances, enemies, and pacts; like any diplomat you can use these to your advantage.

You can use your astrological animal to describe and guide your compatibility with others. Below is a table showing the animal that you are least compatible with and those who are your best friends and allies. You are less likely to get along with the animal directly opposite you in figure 9.1. However if you are working in a partnership with that beast and things are not smooth, you can approach him through an animal who does get along with him—and who has no conflict with you. Communication will now flow better. For example, the Rat's worst enemy is the Horse. If the Rat has to deal with the Horse, then he should bring along a Tiger, Dog, or Ram, as all have good relationships with the Horse.

You need to refer to the animal year table (pages 11–13), to see which animals the people in your workplace or family are. Remember the Chinese solar year starts in February, not January, with the exact start dates for each year noted on the table.

TABLE OF RELATIONSHIPS BETWEEN THE ANIMALS

		SECRET FRIEND	ALLIES	CONFLICTS
Rat		Buffalo	Dragon, Monkey	Horse
Buffalo		Rat	Snake, Rooster	Ram
Tiger		Boar	Horse, Dog	Monkey
Rabbit		Dog	Ram, Boar	Rooster
Dragon		Rooster	Rat, Monkey	Dog
Snake		Monkey	Buffalo, Rooster	Boar
Horse		Ram	Tiger, Dog	Rat
Ram		Horse	Rabbit, Boar	Buffalo

		SECRET FRIEND	ALLIES	CONFLICTS
Monkey		Snake	Rat, Dragon	Tiger
Rooster		Dragon	Buffalo, Snake	Rabbit
Dog		Rabbit	Tiger, Horse	Dragon
Boar		Tiger	Rabbit, Ram	Snake

Notice from figure 9.1 and the table above that the conflict animal is the one diagonally opposite your animal in the circle. The allies are the two animals that are four positions away on either side.

EARTHLY BRANCH LOVE

Love forecasts are a common feature of popular Chinese astrology, which is usually based on animal branches, and indeed these forecasts are always a good subject to attract readers. The animal branches give some further interesting clues and there are also feng shui tips to help find a partner.

Romance is referred to by the charming expression "peach blossom," and there are also relationships within the animal branches that can suggest love is in the air.

As we saw above there are four groups of three animals who get on well together. You will already have a good affinity with the other animals in your group. The groups are:

> Rat, Monkey, and Dragon
> Rabbit, Boar, and Ram
> Horse, Tiger, and Dog
> Rooster, Snake, and Buffalo

There are four animals that are considered to be particularly sexually attractive: one from each group. In fact they represent the four cardinal points of the compass:

> North—Rat
> East—Rabbit
> South—Horse
> West—Rooster

If a person has all four in their birth chart then they would be a very charismatic flirt or have a playboy nature. If you have two or three of these signs and the set is completed during a luck period then the above would also be true for that time period. Their place in the chart and also the chart as a whole would always have to be considered before knowing the effect it has on the person's life.

Using a feng shui tip you could also activate your peach blossom area in your home or workplace. To do this you must first locate your year animal in the above groups. The next step is to locate the directional sector of your house that corresponds to the peach blossom animal in your group. Place a vase of freshly cut flowers there; make sure that the water is clean and the flowers in good condition. You do not want to attract peach blossom of a dirty or faded nature.

You can also leave a symbolic animal of the corresponding color made out of glass, porcelain, or metal in the chosen peach blossom sector: a dark blue Rat in the north, a green Rabbit in the east, a red Horse in the south, or a white Rooster in the west. To be able to decide on the directions in your house you must first take a compass reading from the wall of your house that you consider the front or facing side. There are twelve animal branch directions making up

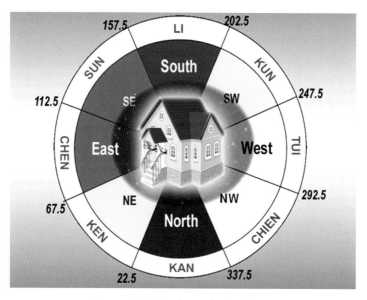

Figure 9.2. Northeast-facing house

the 360° of the compass, so a Chinese compass would be divided into twelve sections. In figure 9.2 the four cardinal directions—north, south, east, and west—are shown based on a northeast facing house with the eight directions on an ordinary compass superimposed on it.

CLASHES AND TRINITIES

There are many special conditions and cases in respect to combinations of elements both within your birth chart and from incoming luck cycles, which we will refer to briefly here. There are phenomena that are potentially harmful and others that bring added benefits to your chart.

Clashes in the Earthly Branches

As we have seen above each animal has a conflict animal. The appearance of this animal in an incoming luck period or even in the birth chart indicates a "clash." Major clashes on the birth chart or in annual or ten-year luck cycles are indicated on your chart in the section titled "10 Years Annual Luck Cycle Details." You can also work out for yourself when the animal diagonally opposite your own comes in, causing a clash (see figure 9.1). The following pairs clash: Rat/Horse, Buffalo/Ram, Tiger/Monkey, Rabbit/Rooster, Dragon/Dog, Snake/Boar. Animal branches can also form other relationships that can be harmful in certain circumstances; these are usually referred to as harms and penalties.

Note the pillars where the clashes in the chart occur, as they affect this area of life. The clashes can be found in the ten-year luck periods as well as calendar years. Clashes affect compatibilities, as explained in element terms below:

1. Yin Water and Yin Fire as Rat and Horse clash. This clash can cause mental disability and, if appearing in the day and year pillars, indicate clash with spouse or relatives. Cure with friends and allies from the animal table on pages 116–17.

2. Yin Earth Buffalo and Yin Earth Ram clash. This clash can indicate problems of buildings collapsing, desert heat, or avalanche and can be balanced with Wood energy.

3. Yang Wood and Yang Metal as Tiger and Monkey clash. It is related to traffic accidents if in ten-year luck period. Balance this out with Water energy.

4. Yin Wood and Yin Metal as Rabbit and Rooster clash. This can be physical accidents affecting the neck. Balance out with Water energy and with heart meditation. This will melt the Metal to flow into the Water.

5. Yang Earth Dragon and Yang Earth Dog clash. This can bring on depression due to pressure; Yang Earth collision can be a tremendous force like an earthquake. Balance with Metal energy.

6. Yang Fire and Yang Water as Snake and Boar clash. This can indicate traffic accidents and misfortunes due to water movement. Protect using friends and allies from animal table on pages 116–17.

Branch Trinities or Super-Elements

There are also conditions of "super-elements" being formed when three elements blend together to form a new one. If these three elements are in your birth chart, or when you put the ten-year and annual luck cycles alongside your birth chart and they come together for that defined period, then a new "super-element" is formed. You must now consider the impact of adding that new element.

Branches: Rat, Dragon, and Monkey together form Water. Boar, Rabbit, and Ram form Wood. Buffalo, Rooster, and Snake form Metal. Tiger, Dog, and Horse form Fire.

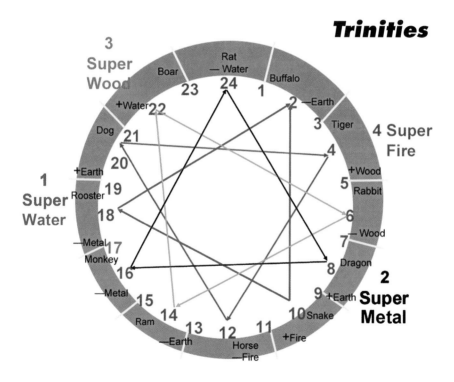

Figure 9.3. Super-elements formed by trinities. The numbers 1–24 denote hours as in the 24-hour clock. Unlike our other uses of the Chinese compass with south at the top and north at the bottom, here we have put north at the top and south at the bottom as in a clock face so that it is more obvious that we are reading the animal branches expressed as time.

Heavenly Stem Clashes

The heavenly stems can also clash: Yang Wood clashes with Yang Metal, Yin Wood clashes with Yin Metal, Yang Fire clashes with Yang Water, and Yin Fire clashes with Yin Water. Although clashes involving Earth element in the branches are strong, Earth clashes do not occur in the heavenly stems.

There are also combinations of heavenly stems that can unite to make another element:

Yang Wood and Yin Earth = Earth
Yang Metal and Yin Wood = Metal
Yang Fire and Yin Metal = Water
Yang Water and Yin Fire = Wood
Yang Earth and Yin Water = Fire

Again these stem transformations may be found in the birth chart or may occur during incoming luck periods. In astrology clashes, trinities, super-elements, and combinations help to explain changes in life energies and events that basic chart reading does not indicate.

How do we balance out these energies? Well, refer to the table on the five elements, emotions, and energies (page 24); it also includes the colors, directions, shapes, body parts, seasons, and planets of these energies. As you are now familiar with the energies you can design your own program using the Inner Alchemy practices and other tools to enhance or weaken an element around you or in you.

Deeper Chart Interpretations

Chinese metaphysics often mentions the "golden mean," a middle way through the excesses of too much or too little, and astrology interpretation is sometimes saying "less is more." We have learned in this book that having a very strong element does not make you a king. Having a strong element automatically means there is less elsewhere, which will mean some weaker or very weak elements. A very strong element can certainly mean an exceptional life for some; their achievements using their strong element energy could be impressive, but there could be an Achilles heel somewhere. This weakness could be revealed at a change in a ten-year luck cycle, or it could be smoothed out by an incoming luck period; a person who was previously finding life difficult could blossom at this point.

The completely balanced chart is impossible. Even if the elements were equally represented as 20 percent each in the birth chart, there would still be the fluctuating ten-year luck cycles that would make one of these elements stronger and others consequently weaker. Inner Alchemy practices, feng shui, and other Taoist arts should be practiced with the idea of balancing your elements and of bringing harmony to your energies.

UNDERSTANDING YOU
AND YOUR FAMILY

Remember that you are the day master situated in the top half of the day pillar. From here you can study the relationship you have or have had with other members of your family and other components of society.

HOW YOUR FAMILY FITS INTO YOUR FOUR PILLARS

	HOUR	DAY	MONTH	YEAR
	Children Workers	Self, Siblings, Peers	Parents, Boss Upbringing	Grandparents Society
Stem	Sons	Self	Father	Grandfather
Branch	Daughters	Marriage, Partner	Mother	Grandmother

Starting from the right with the year pillar (which was formed from the year in which you were born) we can study our relationship with grandparents and also how we fit in with society as a whole. Broadly speaking, the grandfather role is visible in the heavenly stem and the grandmother in the branch.

Men were usually more visible than women in ancient Chinese society, which is why they are often interpreted on the more visible heavenly stem line. Women are then seen in the more hidden branch line. Society today is very different, and even in the past many families had women playing more prominent roles. The cultural setting of the chart is therefore an important consideration. This year pillar also shows how you fit into society as a whole: did (or does) it support, control, or help you? Look at the elements in your own year pillar and see to which phase they correspond (from figures 4.4a–4.4j). According to the ten gods tables, what can you deduce about your relationship with your grandparents or with society as a whole?

Knowledge of the five elements relationships is essential for this interpretation. The key to understanding yourself and the others is to examine the relationship between your day master element and the other elements in the chart (see the table of the ten day masters and the elements representing their ten gods on page 61).

The month pillar, which was formed from the month in which you were born, shows your parents. Again, generally the father is in the stems and the mother in the branches. The most visible part of your life is in the stems; the branches reveal what is more of a foundation to you but is not necessarily there for people to see. A classical view is that a "good" father would be the element that is controlled by your own element, and a "good" mother is the element that nourishes your element.

The day pillar, formed from the actual birth day in conjunction with the month and year, has you in the stem and your spouse in the branches. Here we can read the relationship we have with our spouses or how we see marriage and partners. Do we nurture them? Do they control us? Are they good friends? This pillar also represents our siblings and peers.

The hour pillar represents our children, or rather our relationship to them, and also our senior years. In traditional Chinese society children were responsible for looking after their parents in their later years, which is why this pillar will indicate how the energies in your life will support you then. The hour pillar also represents your employees, your students, or people for whom you are responsible. If your birth time is not correct then reading this pillar is mere speculation. However, in the case of you not knowing your birth time, as long as the other pillars are correct you can already gain a lot of valuable information about the energy in your life from reading them.

If we are looking at the whole chart, children are generally shown in a woman's expression phase element and in a man's wealth phase.

	HOUR	DAY	MONTH	YEAR
Stem	Yin Wood	Yang Fire	Yang Wood	Yin Water
Branch	Ram Yin Earth Yin Fire Yin Wood	Dragon Yang Earth Yin Wood Yin Water	Rat Yin Water	Ram Yin Earth Yin Fire Yin Wood

Figure 10.1a. Linda's birth chart

Make a note of the ten gods on your birth chart as in figure 10.1b.

Looking at Linda's birth chart, we can see a difficult relationship with her father as Yang Wood is hostile resource to her Yang Fire day master. Hostile resource is improper parenting. It could be either something harmful or it could be spoiling a child, which is not necessarily done with harmful intentions but is not in the child's best interests. The Yin Water for the mother suggests a much better relationship, as proper power is organizing the right structure around her, creating a good upbringing.

DAY	MONTH	YEAR
SELF	**PARENTS**	**GRANDPARENTS, SOCIETY**
Yang Fire	**Yang Wood** Hostile Resource	**Yin Water** Proper Power
	Rat **Yin Water** Proper Power	**Ram** **Yin Earth** Opposing Expression **Yin Fire** Unfriendly Self **Yin Wood** Proper Resource

Figure 10.1b. Linda's day, month, and year pillars with ten gods added

Further information from her ten-year luck cycle in figure 10.1c suggests that she suffered harm from her father or from being in his care before the age of ten. The earthly branch energies came in halfway through the luck period, at around four years of age. As it is the same energy as represented by her mother in the birth chart, we could read that she took over and rescued her from this situation. When proper resource comes in at ten, this is even better for her as it is the right sort of parental care and control.

From her grandparents' palace—the year pillar—we can see some nurturing resource in the branches and some proper power in the stem line. Her grandparent could well have stepped in when Linda was about four years of age, when the proper power energy got stronger in the branch line. This power element represents a grandparent.

In the branch line, her grandmother's relationship with her suggests good nurturing (Yin Wood is proper resource) and good company (Yin Fire is friendly self).

	0–9	10–19
Stem	Hostile Resource	Proper Resource
Branch	Proper Power	Opposing Expression Proper Power Proper Wealth

Figure 10.1c. Two of Linda's ten-year luck cycles

	HOUR	DAY
	Children or Employees	Self
Stem	**Yin Wood** Proper Resource	**Yang Fire** Day Master Marriage Palace
Branch	**Ram** **Yin Earth** Opposing Expression **Yin Fire** Unfriendly Self **Yin Wood** Proper Resource	**Dragon** **Yang Earth** Proper Expression **Yin Wood** Proper Resource **Yin Water** Proper Power

Figure 10.1d. Linda's marriage and future life palaces

In her marriage palace, we can see love or some "perfect" compatibility with a husband, as Yin Water is her proper power. She will have good support (Yin Wood is her proper resource), and marriage allows her to work and possibly have children (Yang Earth is her proper expression). Proper expression is also good investment, so we could consider her marriage as that.

Linda's children palace suggests good support, because proper resource appears twice. This palace is also indicative of life in your old age, which of course in traditional Chinese society meant your children should look after you. There is some rivalry (unfriendly self) and possible bad investments or problems with a child (opposing expression).

PREDOMINANT HEAVENLY INFLUENCE

There is one part of your chart that could be read as "what makes you tick." It indicates a phase that you strive toward more than the others; it is your deeper motivation. This predominant heavenly influence is stronger on you than the other phases' influence, but you might not be aware of it as being your deeper purpose. It is quite likely to be confirmed by the way you live and spend your time.

It is read in the month branch. Which phase does this element correspond to for you? Is it your expression, wealth, power, resource, or friend phase?

Expression: We can say that your output at work, your art, writing, speaking, or children are of particular importance and even a preoccupation for you.

Wealth: Obviously a lot of people are driven by money. It can represent something you own and collect, like an art collection, something you control, or something of intellectual value as well as material value. For a man it can also be love, women, his wife, or achievements.

Power: This can mean fitting in, rising in rank or promotions, and obviously having power over others. For women it can be their husband, or finding one.

Resource: Being taken care of, having a support "behind you," investing for "your old age," and also education.

Friends: Your social life, peer group, siblings, you and your thoughts, self-justification, and self-analysis.

	HOUR	DAY	MONTH	YEAR
Stem	Yin Wood	Yang Fire	Yang Wood	Yin Water
Branch	Ram Yin Earth Yin Fire Yin Wood	Dragon Yang Earth Yin Wood Yin Water	Rat **Yin Water**	Ram Yin Earth Yin Fire Yin Wood

Figure 10.2. Linda's birth chart, with her predominant heavenly influence shown in bold

Linda's predominant heavenly influence is her power phase, as it is Water and she is a Fire day master.

Notice that she also has Yin Water in her stem line. The three other stems are things that are easy to see about yourself. In this example, her power phase, her husband is not far from her in life. Yin Wood, her proper resource, is the hour pillar stem right next to her. She would probably have a very close relationship with her mother. The other stem is Yang Wood: she would remain close to her father, stepfather, or father figure.

To calculate the predominant heavenly influence for yourself look at your month pillar in the bottom line, the earthly branch. As we have seen before, some animals have only one element and some have further hidden elements. If there is only one element here then that is the predominant heavenly influence. You know what phase that is for you, and so you can judge how much that "makes you tick."

If there is more than one element in your month animal, start with the first and check it against the day stem (i.e., day master element). If it is the same, try the second, then third on the list to find one that is not the same as the day element but that is also present in another stem (top line). If neither of these apply, then it is the first one. This is calculated for you in the complete Inner Alchemy astrology chart.

In the case of Constance, the predominant heavenly influence is Earth, her power phase. This also represents a high energy element for her; she would spend a lot of time doing the things represented by Earth and her power phase.

	HOUR	DAY	MONTH	YEAR
Stem	Yang Earth	Yang Water	Yin Fire	Yin Earth
Branch	Monkey Yang Metal Yang Earth Yang Water	Horse Yin Fire Yin Earth	Buffalo **Yin Earth** Yin Water Yin Metal	Ram Yin Earth Yin Fire Yin Wood

Figure 10.3a. Constance's birth chart, with her predominant heavenly influence shown in bold

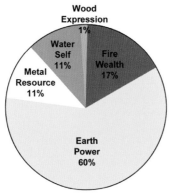

Figure 10.3b. Constance's element percentages

What can you do with this information? You cannot change the facts here. However, it is interesting to know and will possibly help you understand your loved ones better and illuminate the reasons you do all the things you do. You might want to try to resist these tendencies at times in order to get something necessary done.

Knowledge of your chart will help you put more energy into a different phase of your chart, such as to support a particular element energy and bring it into balance. Constance, in the example above, has a very strong power phase; this provides her with many capabilities but also means that she is weaker elsewhere. She should support her Water day master more and also her Wood element to improve energy flow to Fire, her wealth phase. This would enable her to achieve more real wealth or success, improve her organ health, and feel more fulfilled in her own day master desires.

	HOUR	DAY	MONTH	YEAR
Stem	Yin Metal	Yang Water	Yin Fire	Yang Metal
Branch	Buffalo Yin Earth Yin Water Yin Metal	Tiger Yang Wood Yang Fire Yang Earth	Boar **Yang Water** Yang Wood	Horse Yin Fire Yin Earth

Figure 10.4a. Jay's birth chart, with his predominant heavenly influence shown in bold

Jay's predominant heavenly influence is Water, or friends phase. He is a strong Water day master but has weaker expression, wealth,

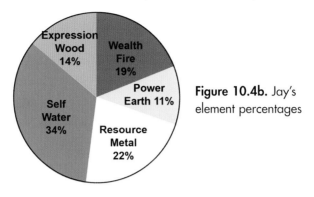

Figure 10.4b. Jay's element percentages

and power phases. These phases are not very weak, but resisting his social life or a desire to philosophize and "putting himself into his work," by concentrating more on expression, would improve the flow of energy to his wealth. Wealth of course can mean many things to many people. It is not just monetary: it can represent academic degrees, knowledge, and a wife for a man. The flow of energy around the elements also strengthens the organs and the physical body, and therefore the health.

June's day master is Yang Fire; her predominant heavenly influence is Metal or her wealth phase. As her Metal energy is not very large it does not indicate great achievement for this phase; it is a preoccupation for her that would be a great frustration and worry. The Inner Smile meditation would help energy flow from her very strong day master through her expression phase to her wealth phase. Her power phase also needs some bolstering; it could mean insufficient self-discipline to achieve things that this very strong Fire energy could do easily—if she would focus and not just act "fiery."

	HOUR	DAY	MONTH	YEAR
Stem	Yin Metal	Yang Fire	Yin Wood	Yin Fire
Branch	Rabbit Yin Wood	Dog Yang Earth Yin Metal Yin Fire	Snake Yang Fire Yang Earth **Yang Metal**	Boar Yang Water Yang Wood

Figure 10.5a. June's birth chart,
with her predominant heavenly influence shown in bold

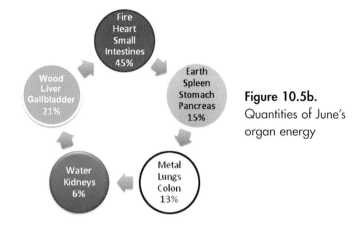

Figure 10.5b.
Quantities of June's organ energy

LOVE INTEREST

When your "love interest" element appears in your annual or ten-year luck cycle, you can expect some activity in this part of your life. For a man, his wife would be his wealth element, and for a woman her husband would be her power element. Ideally they would be of the opposite polarity. For example, for a male Yang Metal day master, his "ideal wife" would be a lady Yin Wood day master.

From the marriage palace we can see what a person could well expect from marriage.

From Tracy's marriage palace we can see that her marriage would involve real love with her ideal husband, Yin Fire, and that their relationship might give her great companionship. However, the presence of Yin Metal shows they might have some rivalry, and also some troubled times are shown by Yang Earth. But overall the palace is suggesting true love. That hostile resource (Yang Earth) could be expressed in differences with her husband, not always agreeing with her or being exactly what she wants. This does not mean that it will be a bad marriage at all. We would have to look at the quantities and qualities of both of their elements to really know. In the case of a person who marries several times, then we could conclude that the first marriage was troublesome but the rest more promising.

	HOUR	DAY	MONTH	YEAR
Stem	**Yang Earth** Hostile Resource	**Yang Metal**	**Yin Earth** Proper Resource	**Yin Metal** Unfriendly Self
Branch	**Tiger** **Yang Wood** Extra Wealth **Yang Fire** Hostile Power **Yang Earth** Hostile Resource	**Dog** **Yang Earth** Hostile Resource **Yin Metal** Unfriendly Self **Yin Fire** Proper Power	**Boar** **Yang Water** Proper Expression **Yang Wood** Extra Wealth	**Boar** **Yang Water** Proper Expression **Yang Wood** Extra Wealth

Figure 10.6a. Tracy's birth chart

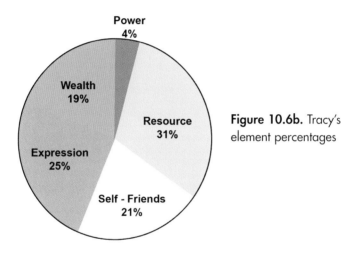

Figure 10.6b. Tracy's element percentages

Tracy is a normal-sized Yang Metal person whose predominant heavenly influence is her expression; her chart can show a very artistic person or a great communicator. Her weakest element is her power phase, which can mean a lack of organization or an anarchistic streak. Power is also her husband element. Looking at their charts together would give more information on their relationship, compatibilities, and incompatibilities. Healing disruptive energies through Taoist techniques would create more harmony and smooth over more challenging energies in her marriage palace. Life is a cycle of changes as ten-year luck and annual luck periods come and go; a long-term marriage would generally encounter challenging energies at some point. Many people advise "working on a marriage"; there are many Taoist tools to make the difficult times more harmonious.

From your marriage palace and your life up to now, you will see what love and marriage brings to you; such relationships mean different things to different people. The energies described in the marriage palace suggest that a style of relationship will work for some and not for others.

If your day master is very strong or very weak then prospective partners with a compatible day master element must be able to fit well for things to work. A very large Water day master man could drown a weak Fire girlfriend. In fact that would fizzle out so quickly that it would not really be a long-term contender, and the initial attraction would not be likely. When day masters are of exceptional size then partnerships are often formed with a day master who is not of the "ideal" husband or wife element. Only by looking at the quantities of the elements will you be able to understand how the relationship works. However, having the ideal element appear in the dynamic luck periods would probably indicate when there was romance energy around. There is also animal branch love compatibility and the peach blossom effect to consider as discussed in the previous chapter.

PREVENTION IS ALWAYS BETTER THAN A CURE

An advantage of Taoist astrology is that it tells you how to correct things. It quickly pinpoints what is going to happen in terms of elements coming into your chart, which means influencing your life, over your lifetime.

In the same way that you prepare for winter by checking the heating, filling up with fuel, and getting out warm clothes, you can prepare for the advent of a "difficult" cycle and think what you can do to mitigate it.

Less favorable energies will at some point come in for a year or ten years, attacking one of the five elements. Be aware of what phase these elements represent for you; for example, if it is your expression phase that will be attacked then it might not be the right time to put a lot of money, energy, and work into making an investment.

If it is your wealth phase then pay attention to difficulties in your marriage if you are a man, or to your actual wealth or what you control for both sexes. If it is your power phase then you could find problems with the hierarchy at work, or if you are a woman it could be your marriage or relationship. If it is your self element then watch your health and be more careful with your diet and lifestyle. Use the practices as you would use preventive medicine.

Start preventive strategies with your birth chart. Strengthen the weaker elements as explained in chapters 1–7 in this book. If you do the practices and meditations during the season corresponding to the element and also the time corresponding to the organ meridian, you will be taking advantage of those energies when they are at their highest potential. Then continue preventive Chi Kung and meditations according to the incoming attacking energies.

ORGANS AND OTHER PARTS OF THE BODY	TIME FOR MERIDIAN	ELEMENT	SEASON
Gallbladder Eyes, Tear Ducts, Tendons, Nails, Bile Production	11 p.m.–1 a.m. (2300–0100 hrs.)	Yang Wood	Spring
Liver Eyes, Tear Ducts, Tendons, Nails	1 a.m.–3 a.m. (0100–0300 hrs.)	Yin Wood	Spring
Lungs Nose, Mucus, Skin, Body Hair	3 a.m.–5 a.m. (0300–0500 hrs.)	Yin Metal	Autumn/Fall
Large Intestine Nose, Mucus, Skin, Body Hair	5 a.m.–7 a.m. (0500–0700 hrs.)	Yang Metal	Autumn/Fall

ORGANS AND OTHER PARTS OF THE BODY	TIME FOR MERIDIAN	ELEMENT	SEASON
Stomach	7 a.m.–9 a.m. (0700–0900 hrs.)	Yang Earth	Indian Summer
Spleen and Pancreas Saliva, Lymphatic Glands, Mouth	9 a.m.–11 a.m. (0900–1100 hrs.)	Yin Earth	Indian Summer
Heart Tongue, Blood System Glands: thyroids, adrenals, prostate, pituitary	11 a.m.–1 p.m. (1100–1300 hrs.)	Yin Fire	Summer
Small Intestines Tongue, Blood System, Sweat	1 p.m.–3 p.m. (1300–1500 hrs.)	Yang Fire	Summer
Bladder Urine System	3 p.m.–5 p.m. (1500–1700 hrs.)	Yang Water	Winter
Kidneys Ears and Hearing, Bones, Urine, Head and Body Hair, Brains	5 p.m.–7 p.m. (1700–1900 hrs.)	Yin Water	Winter
Pericardium Blood System, Throat	7 p.m.–9 p.m. (1900–2100 hrs.)	Yin Fire	Summer
Triple Warmer Cooling and Bodily Fluid Flow	9 p.m.–11 p.m. (2100–2300 hrs.)	Yang Fire	Summer

Figure 10.7. Organs and other parts of the body

TAO OF FORGIVENESS

You have identified what each of the ten gods represents for you and have determined when they will come into your life as part of your luck cycles. In order of risk, the most difficult phases are hostile power and hostile resource; then less harmful but with potential consequences are unfriendly self, opposing expression, and extra wealth. When you have challenging energy coming toward you, it can be better to meet it head on. The effects are of course completely dependent on the strength of your day master and other elements in your chart.

To help yourself learn to identify the relationship between your chart and your experiences, examine which events in your past correspond to hostile power and hostile resource. If these phases are in your month pillar then you should be able to identify events that occurred during your childhood and adolescent years. If you find them in a ten-year luck cycle, then challenging events would have happened during those ten years. As we look toward the future, we can effectively take the "sting" out of these approaching energies by wrapping them in loving forgiveness.

Energy of Forgiveness

To avoid future or present problems with relationships you must work on the energy of the problem. If you have felt the pain in the past then it is easy to visualize. If we look closely at our next example, we can see that Martha's parents personify hostile resource and hostile power. This is useful as, in Martha's case, it gives us an image of her parents and painful events experienced with them. She can visualize her parents and send loving, forgiving energy. She would work on forgiveness and letting go of any resentment toward her father and mother for what might have taken place. The energy of forgiveness will disarm the harmful elements and leave them no place to go within you in the future. It is the equivalent of removing the address programmed in the satellite-navigation system of these difficult energies so they will not be able to return.

	HOUR	DAY/SELF	MONTH/PARENTS	YEAR
Stem	Yin Wood	Yin Fire	Yin Wood	Yang Earth
	Hostile Resource		Hostile Resource	Opposing Expression
Branch	**Snake** **Yang Fire** Unfriendly Self **Yang Earth** Opposing Expression **Yang Metal** Proper Wealth	**Snake** **Yang Fire** Unfriendly Self **Yang Earth** Opposing Expression **Yang Metal** Proper Wealth	**Buffalo** **Yin Earth** Proper Expression **Yin Water** Hostile Power **Yin Metal** Extra Wealth	**Rat** **Yin Water** Hostile Power

Figure 10.8a. Martha's birth chart, normal strength Yin Fire day master

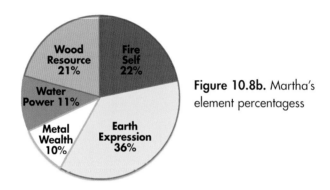

Figure 10.8b. Martha's element percentagess

As a child Martha did indeed experience poor parenting and poor relationships with her parents. We can see hostile resource in her parent palace stem (i.e., her month pillar) and there is also hostile power down in the branches and from at least one grandparent.

Her predominant heavenly influence is expression; it is a large phase for her and explains why she works very hard and has reached a high managerial position. Such large Earth has given her very good organizational and management skills, and her chart fits her work in a humanitarian organization. As her wealth phase is relatively weak, it follows that she has a very high, honorary position in an international organization rather than in the well-paid commercial world. As a normal strength Fire person, she is a naturally charismatic well-known speaker, bringing her passion to her work.

	0–6 YEARS	7–16 YEARS	17–26 YEARS
Stem	**Yin Wood** Hostile Resource	**Yang Wood** Proper Resource	**Yin Water** Hostile Power
Branch	**Buffalo** **Yin Earth** Proper Expression **Yin Water** Hostile Power **Yin Metal** Extra Wealth	**Rat** **Yin Water** Hostile Power	**Boar** **Yang Water** Proper Power **Yang Wood** Proper Resource

Figure 10.8c. Extract from Martha's
ten-year luck cycles

	2011	2012	2013
Stem	**Yin Metal** Extra Wealth	**Yang Water** Proper Power	**Yin Water** Hostile Power
Branch	**Rabbit** **Yin Wood** Hostile Resource	**Dragon** **Yang Earth** Opposing Expression **Yin Wood** Hostile Resource **Yin Water** Hostile Power	**Snake** **Yang Fire** Unfriendly Self **Yang Earth** Opposing Expression **Yang Metal** Proper Wealth

Figure 10.8d. Three years of Martha's annual luck

We can glean further information from her parents' palace (the month pillar in the natal chart) by examining her early ten-year luck periods. From birth to the age of six years, the hostile resource in the stem line describes the relationship she had with her father: an uninvolved, distant parent. The hostile power would be from the relationship with her mother who left her in difficult situations where she was blamed for many problems within the family.

However, from seven to eleven years was a better time for her as there was someone more helpful involved in her upbringing, in the form of proper resource, as the new ten-year luck period started. She suffered much difficulty when the earthly branch energies—hostile power—became stronger halfway through the ten years. This continued until around twenty-two years of age, when she was old enough to leave home. After age twenty-six her ten-year luck cycles continue in a more opportune manner. Her worst period was during her early childhood.

The annual luck energy (figure 10.8d) is the same for everybody, but what it represents depends on your day master and which of the ten gods are represented by the yearly energy. For Martha, we can see that she once again will have hostile resource and hostile power to contend with during the years 2010–2013. However, as it is not repeated in her ten-year luck period during that time, it will not be as bad.

Practicing the Tao of Forgiveness

For Martha the Yin Wood hostile resource energy is symbolized by her father and their relationship when she was a child, and events that occurred due to this. But Martha can meet this energy head on by using the techniques of the Tao of Forgiveness, the Taoist practices that are aimed at forgiving and therefore disarming the harmful element energy. During the Inner Smile meditation, or when using the technique from time to time outside the meditations, she should put an image of her father in front of her and go back to the pain and events surrounding her relationship with him.

The hostile resource energy in this example is Wood, so her practice will be stronger if she goes to the east of the house or room, or turns to face the direction east. With much sincerity, she must tell her father that she loves him and she forgives him. With hands near her heart, she must smile into her heart and smile sincerely with love and compassion, together with forgiveness, then let go of what happened and smile to her father. For very painful memories, it is necessary to do the delete-key rapid eye movement exercise, as taught in Supreme Inner Alchemy basic practices. This technique weakens and eventually deletes negative emotions stored in the organs, but it does not delete the persons or the memories of the persons involved.

Martha's hostile power phase is the Water element. She should turn to the north and smile to the blue energy of Water, and smile into her heart and toward her mother. With complete sincerity she must forgive her and let go of the bad memories and the pain. Smiling to the heart to let go of the pain will free up space within her to be filled by the good and positive emotions of the organs.

If you continue to feel memories as painful and see the incoming hostile resource and hostile power energy as painful and harmful, then that leaves the energy a place to go inside of you. Leaving a spot for this energy is essentially giving it an address to go to, and it could well be harmful and painful for you. Mantak Chia explains in his Inner Smile meditation seminars that when you smile to your heart and send love, joy, and compassion, it is as if you are giving the universal energies the address, telephone number, or e-mail address of your body organ. The energies are there for you to tune in to, and you can help by using your smile, the corresponding element color, and its direction. If you keep fear, resentment, hurt, or other negative

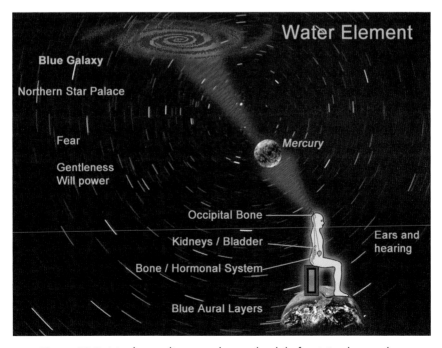

Figure 10.9. Martha meditates to the north while forgiving her mother.

emotions in this place then the incoming negative energy also has the address and a place to go where it will feel at home.

Ancient cultures were much more in touch with universal energies and sky-watching than the man-in-the-street is today. Our Taoist practices have elements in common with other ancient culture's practices. The Taoist meditation of forgiveness is similar to another ancient practice, Hawaiian *ho'oponopono*.

The practice involves working on yourself to solve problems outside of you. In ho'oponopono you put problems right by addressing the source of problems within you and cleansing yourself with maxims: "I am sorry," "please forgive me," "I love you," and "thank you." The concept is similar to Taoist techniques as it works on sorting out energy—forgiving and letting go, in order to settle family or other relationship problems and even illnesses. Ancient Hawaiians, too, saw the connection between man and the cosmos and talked of "gods" who personified nature, such as Pele, the goddess of fire, and her sister the goddess of water.

In ancient times these rituals were performed by priests, although the family was involved. Universal Healing Tao practices do not involve working with a priest, although doing the exercises in a group with a teacher is quite common.

One thing is clear: replacing harmful and painful memories with positive thoughts and emotions creates an environment that will attract more positives and will not allow the negatives to move into those places and harm you. Like our example, we can repeat this exercise over and over, practicing the delete-key rapid eye movement exercise and the Inner Smile to the element.

The other positive outcome for Martha could be an improvement in the relationship with her father, if he is still alive. If he is no longer there then the pain of the difficult relationship will fade for her. More than anything, the pain of a difficult relationship happening again could be avoided by this exercise. The hostile resource coming into Martha's life is in fact just an energy; by this Taoist practice of forgiveness she is negating the energy and rendering it harmless—or less harmful. Remember the intention in the three treasures of heaven, earth, and human. Intention and sincerity can be worked on to avoid, downscale, or help you to better cope with problems.

TAO OF ABUNDANCE

Many books and therapies have lately been available on the "law of attraction," stemming mainly from the release of the film *The Secret*. The film focused on this law as the most powerful one in the universe, and it is revealed as being a common truth that is at the core of the most powerful philosophies and religions in the world. Well, yes, Taoists have always known about the law of attraction and the nature of abundance. Taoist practices have involved tuning one's own vibration to the cosmic energies in the universe and changing one's negative emotions into positive energy.

When there is so much truth in this law, how do we explain the failure of the many who have tried these methods, either by creating a visual wish list of things they would like to obtain or by trying to change their thought vibrations to positive?

Five-element astrology shows that people have very different astrological makeups and are affected by the energies of the universe in different ways. Many people ask for wealth, but wealth energy is not the same for everybody. It is dependent on your day master and also on the quantity and quality of your other elements. Remember that it is difficult to obtain wealth possibilities without a good expression energy (i.e., no work, no gain), which in turn needs some support from the day master. Partners in a marriage or company could have different wealth elements, which would mean that wealth has different implications for each of them, and likewise they would have differing opinions on investments.

This is why blanket methods for attracting wealth will not work for everybody. Nor will methods for attracting love or sorting your life out in other ways be applicable for everyone. At the most, the energy of the day or year will be the appropriate wealth energy for one out of ten people, and even then the condition of their birth chart—particularly their day master and expression energy—would come into the equation. And let us not forget which ten-year luck period they are presently in, and what the annual and daily luck means to them.

For example, if Earth is your wealth energy then it could be counted in property. If Metal is your wealth then the more traditional money or jewels would be appropriate. The ten-year luck periods show what major changes in energy will be coming into your life, and annual and daily energy calculations will show what energy is coming to everyone on the planet. After studying your chart and the luck periods you must work out what that annual or daily energy means to you: what phases these energies represent, which of the ten gods they are for you, and what their arrival means to the balance of your chart.

Our example, June, is a very strong Yang Fire day master and her predominant heavenly influence is Metal, her wealth phase. As her Metal energy is not very large it does not indicate great achievement for this phase, which would be a great frustration and worry to her. The Inner Smile meditation would help energy flow from her very strong day master through her expression phase to her wealth phase. Her power phase also needs some bolstering, as it does not give her enough self-discipline to enable this very strong Fire energy to achieve what it is capable of.

If June wishes to concentrate on the law of attraction or Tao of abundance techniques, she could also choose appropriate times to do so. As figure 10.10c shows, her ten-year luck cycle has proper wealth coming in, probably from her work and projects. So her wealth is really available. This desirable energy for her starts as soon as the luck period starts, although the earthly energies of hostile power and hostile resource will become stronger at around four to five years into the period. So she must also work on those negative energies with the tools of love and forgiveness to avoid them disabling the great potential of these ten years.

	HOUR	DAY	MONTH	YEAR
Stem	Yin Metal	**Yang Fire**	Yin Wood	Yin Fire
Branch	Rabbit Yin Wood	Dog Yang Earth Yin Metal Yin Fire	Snake Yang Fire Yang Earth **Yang Metal**	Boar Yang Water Yang Wood

Figure 10.10a. June's birth chart

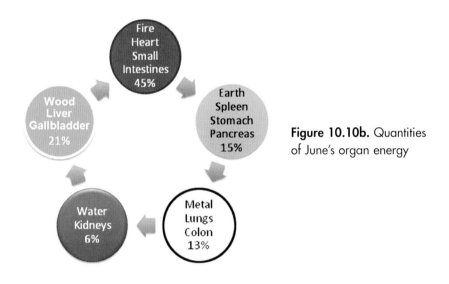

Figure 10.10b. Quantities of June's organ energy

TEN-YEAR LUCK CYCLE	
Stem	**Yin Metal** Proper Wealth
Branch	**Boar** **Yang Water** Hostile Power **Yang Wood** Hostile Resource

Figure 10.10c. June's current ten-year luck cycle

Looking at how annual luck will affect her we see that, again, there is wealth available for June. The year 2010 has extra wealth, which is usually less to do with results of regular work but more in the nature of a windfall or something unexpected. She must be aware of and try to deflect the relationship problems that could come in from the hostile resource. There is some proper expression, bolstering her relatively weak expression; this would help her work for the very good proper wealth due to come into her life in 2011.

	2010	2011
Stem	**Yang Metal** Extra Wealth	**Yin Metal** Proper Wealth
Branch	**Tiger** **Yang Wood** Hostile Resource **Yang Earth** Proper Expression	**Rabbit** **Yin Wood** Proper Resource

Figure 10.10d. June's lucky years

	2012	2013
Stem	**Yang Water** Hostile Power	**Yin Water** Proper Power
Branch	**Dragon** **Yang Earth** Proper Expression **Yin Wood** Proper Resource **Yin Water** Proper Power	**Snake** **Yang Fire** Friendly Self **Yang Earth** Proper Expression **Yang Metal** Extra Wealth

Figure 10.10e. Two years of June's annual luck

Another thing that June would have on her wish list is a new relationship and hopefully marriage. Divorced a few years ago, she would like to rebuild her life with someone. Her Yang Fire day master is very strong, which makes it more difficult to form a relationship with her "ideal" Yin Water husband. This is because a Yin Water husband would have to have a very strong day master in order not to be consumed by this Fire. Her previous husband was Metal; her strong Fire day master could control him, but she suffered the frustrations of feeling that he did not look after her as she feels a husband should.

However, the years 2012 and 2013 (shown in figure 10.10e) are both years of her ideal husband element. Yang Water brings her hostile power: possibly "the wrong man" or misfortune in that area. But toward the end of the year there is proper power, meaning ideal husband material, followed by more proper power, which is the heavenly stem energy of 2013.

There is potential abundance in these two areas of June's life, the very two areas that she would place on her vision board. But there are conditions necessary for her to achieve them. She must deal with the hostile resource and hostile power, which could pose problems in four or five years time. She must work on loving and forgiving energy and on letting go of past resentments and pain.

She should do the Healing Sounds to balance out her five elements and use the Inner Smile meditation to move energy around her phases. These practices will create the right conditions to receive the answers to the requests she is making to the universe for financial stability and a loving husband. She can also be aware that the daily energy cycle means that the "right" energy for a particular phase comes around every ten days: so if she chooses a more appropriate day to work on that particular energy then she would be more likely to realize her wishes.

Thinking positive and focusing on what you want to achieve is of course a good thing—but focusing on the element qualities of your own wealth energy is more likely to bring wealth results. Another factor that can increase success is exercising this focus during the more fortunate luck periods, when the elements that favor the desired results are present for you. If your day master is weak then supporting it is essential to give it the strength it needs to seize the wealth. If your expression and wealth elements are weak use the Inner Smile meditation to move energy around to support them. Understanding your astrological chart would be an aid in this project, especially when practicing Inner Alchemy meditations.

Everything is energy; we are made up of energy. Taoist astrology theory is a way of describing the quality and quantity of energy that forms us. People, in their brains and in their physical bodies, are so different in size and performance from each other. Likewise their "energy" makeup is different, and the ways in which they draw abundance must be specifically matched to them.

TAO OF TOOLS: THE INTANGIBLE HEALING THE TANGIBLE

We have talked about many different practices you can use to balance the energies that are part of your birth chart or are present during a particular luck cycle.

Taoism has given us many tools for improvement. If you look again at the table of the five elements and their correlations on page 24, you will see that it covers a universe that is both tangible and intangible. For example, the Fire element is the energy for love, joy, happiness, yet it is also the energy that corresponds to your heart and small intestines. When working on an element energy level you con-

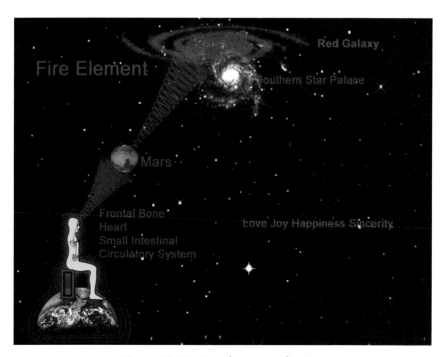

Figure 10.11. Fire element meditation

stantly cross the boundary between physical, or material, and immaterial, intangible energy.

In the Inner Smile meditation we send love, joy, and happiness to the heart. Although this is intangible, it is real; this energy sent to the heart will improve the heart's physical state, which is tangible. You can expect real physical effects from these meditations.

We are going from "love," the nonphysical, to something that is physically material—the body organ, the heart. We no longer have to prove the connection between emotions or energies and the physical health of the body. Western medicine has accepted for some time that stress contributes to illness in a physical form. It has more recently accepted that intangible methods can improve a condition. Meditation and acupuncture are more and more commonly available as state-funded therapies. The right meditation practices can contribute to well-being in its physical form. Meditation rather than medication is an age-old Taoist experience.

Your Taoist astrological chart is a vital tool for understanding your life, past and future. The five elements and the yin and the yang are the foundation for Taoist theory on everything in the universe, of which you are a part. You are now aware of your own five-element makeup and can calculate which elements you need to support the most. The more advanced portions of this book explain which energies will be coming into your destiny and at what moments, together with the directions to meditate in and the useful energies that you can pull down from the universal force. Inner Alchemy astrology teaches you to use Taoist Inner Alchemy practices to enhance and harmonize your own life.

Appendix A
Reference Tables

Below are several useful reference tables from throughout the book. Now that you understand the basics of interpreting your birth chart, you can use this appendix for easy access while working on your own chart interpretations whether you are using a Universal Tao astrological chart, a self-calculated chart, or a chart from another Chinese astrology program. Beneath each table title is a cross-reference to the section of the book that addresses the content of that table. This will allow you to easily return to more in depth information and examples if needed.

SIXTY-YEAR CYCLE OF STEMS AND BRANCHES
(SEE "TAOISTS CONCEPT OF TIME," PAGES 9–14)

	60-YEAR CYCLE YEARS 1924–1983	HEAVENLY STEM	EARTHLY BRANCH	60-YEAR CYCLE 1984–2043
1	Feb 05 1924	Yang Wood	Rat	1984
2	Feb 04 1925	Yin Wood	Buffalo	1985
3	Feb 04 1926	Yang Fire	Tiger	1986
4	Feb 05 1927	Yin Fire	Rabbit	1987
5	Feb 05 1928	Yang Earth	Dragon	1988
6	Feb 04 1929	Yin Earth	Snake	1989
7	Feb 04 1930	Yang Metal	Horse	1990
8	Feb 05 1931	Yin Metal	Ram	1991
9	Feb 05 1932	Yang Water	Monkey	1992

	60-YEAR CYCLE YEARS 1924–1983	HEAVENLY STEM	EARTHLY BRANCH	60-YEAR CYCLE 1984–2043
10	Feb 04 1933	Yin Water	Rooster	1993
11	Feb 04 1934	Yang Wood	Dog	1994
12	Feb 05 1935	Yin Wood	Boar	1995
13	Feb 05 1936	Yang Fire	Rat	1996
14	Feb 04 1937	Yin Fire	Buffalo	1997
15	Feb 04 1938	Yang Earth	Tiger	1998
16	Feb 05 1939	Yin Earth	Rabbit	1999
17	Feb 05 1940	Yang Metal	Dragon	2000
18	Feb 04 1941	Yin Metal	Snake	2001
19	Feb 04 1942	Yang Water	Horse	2002
20	Feb 05 1943	Yin Water	Ram	2003
21	Feb 05 1944	Yang Wood	Monkey	2004
22	Feb 04 1945	Yin Wood	Rooster	2005
23	Feb 04 1946	Yang Fire	Dog	2006
24	Feb 04 1947	Yin Fire	Boar	2007
25	Feb 05 1948	Yang Earth	Rat	2008
26	Feb 04 1949	Yin Earth	Buffalo	2009
27	Feb 04 1950	Yang Metal	Tiger	2010
28	Feb 04 1951	Yin Metal	Rabbit	2011
29	Feb 05 1952	Yang Water	Dragon	2012
30	Feb 04 1953	Yin Water	Snake	2013
31	Feb 04 1954	Yang Wood	Horse	2014
32	Feb 04 1955	Yin Wood	Ram	2015
33	Feb 05 1956	Yang Fire	Monkey	2016
34	Feb 04 1957	Yin Fire	Rooster	2017
35	Feb 04 1958	Yang Earth	Dog	2018

	60-YEAR CYCLE YEARS 1924–1983	HEAVENLY STEM	EARTHLY BRANCH	60-YEAR CYCLE 1984–2043
36	Feb 04 1959	Yin Earth	Boar	2019
37	Feb 05 1960	Yang Metal	Rat	2020
38	Feb 04 1961	Yin Metal	Buffalo	2021
39	Feb 04 1962	Yang Water	Tiger	2022
40	Feb 04 1963	Yin Water	Rabbit	2023
41	Feb 05 1964	Yang Wood	Dragon	2024
42	Feb 04 1965	Yin Wood	Snake	2025
43	Feb 04 1966	Yang Fire	Horse	2026
44	Feb 04 1967	Yin Fire	Ram	2027
45	Feb 05 1968	Yang Earth	Monkey	2028
46	Feb 04 1969	Yin Earth	Rooster	2029
47	Feb 04 1970	Yang Metal	Dog	2030
48	Feb 04 1971	Yin Metal	Boar	2031
49	Feb 05 1972	Yang Water	Rat	2032
50	Feb 04 1973	Yin Water	Buffalo	2033
51	Feb 04 1974	Yang Wood	Tiger	2034
52	Feb 04 1975	Yin Wood	Rabbit	2035
53	Feb 05 1976	Yang Fire	Dragon	2036
54	Feb 04 1977	Yin Fire	Snake	2037
55	Feb 04 1978	Yang Earth	Horse	2038
56	Feb 04 1979	Yin Earth	Ram	2039
57	Feb 05 1980	Yang Metal	Monkey	2040
58	Feb 04 1981	Yin Metal	Rooster	2041
59	Feb 04 1982	Yang Water	Dog	2042
60	Feb 04 1983	Yin Water	Boar	2043

FIVE ELEMENTS, EMOTIONS, AND ORGANS

	FIRE	EARTH	METAL	WATER	WOOD
Yin Organ	Heart	Spleen	Lungs	Kidneys	Liver
Yang Organ	Small Intestines	Pancreas, Stomach	Large Intestine	Bladder	Gallbladder
Sense Organ	Tongue	Mouth, Lips	Nose	Ears	Eyes
Body Parts and Tissues	Blood Circulation System	Armpits, Inner Arms, Muscles	Chest, Skin	Bones, Sexual Organs	Tendons
Positive Emotions	Love, Joy, Happiness, Sincerity	Fairness, Openness, Trust, Justice	Courage, Righteousness	Gentleness, Willpower, Alertness	Generosity, Kindness, Self-Confidence
Negative Emotions	Arrogance, Hastiness, Cruelty, Impatience	Worry, Anxiety	Sadness, Grief, Depression	Fear, Phobias	Anger, Aggression, Jealousy, Envy, Frustration
Color	Red, Purple	Yellow, Beige, Brown	White, Gold, Metal	Black, Dark Blue	Green, Light Blue
Season	Summer	Indian Summer	Fall/Autumn	Winter	Spring
Direction	South	Center	West	North	East
Taste	Bitter	Sweet	Spicy	Salty	Sour
Energy	Radiating	Stabilizing	Contracting	Gathering	Growing
Shape	Triangle	Square	Round	Wavy Lines, Running Lines	Vertical Rectangle
Planet	Mars	Saturn	Venus	Mercury	Jupiter
Planet	Mars	Saturn	Venus	Mercury	Jupiter

TEN GODS EQUIVALENT TERMS
(SEE "NOTE REGARDING TEN GODS TERMS," PAGE 51)

INNER ALCHEMY ASTROLOGY TERMS	ZIPING TERMS (OLDER TERMS)	CHINESE TERMS
Friendly Self	Friends, Self/Friends	比肩
Unfriendly Self	Competitive Self	劫财
Proper Expression	Proper Expression	食神
Opposing Expression	Powerful Expression	伤官
Proper Wealth	Primary Wealth	正财
Extra Wealth	Dynamic Wealth	偏财
Proper Power	Proper Power	正官
Hostile Power	Aggressive Power	七杀
Proper Resource	Primary Resource	正印
Hostile Resource	Inconsistent Resource	偏印

FIND YOUR OWN TEN GODS—TABLES

Note that in these tables, the left column is the day master and the relationship expressed in the grid is the relationship that the element in the top line has with the day master. For example, in the first table (figure 4.4a, Yang Metal day master) when Yang Fire comes in it effectively attacks the day master, which is known as hostile power. The relationships between the day master and the other elements are different for each day master. The "gods" in blue are the most desirable, those in red are the most challenging, and those in black are slightly challenging. (See pages 54–57 for more background information.)

YANG METAL DAY MASTER

	+ Fire	+ Earth	+ Metal	+ Water	+ Wood
+ Metal	Hostile Power	Hostile Resource	Friendly Self	Proper Expression	Extra Wealth
	- Fire	**- Earth**	**- Metal**	**-Water**	**- Wood**
+ Metal	Proper Power	Proper Resource	Unfriendly Self	Opposing Expression	Proper Wealth

YIN METAL DAY MASTER

	+ Fire	+ Earth	+ Metal	+ Water	+ Wood
- Metal	Proper Power	Proper Resource	Unfriendly Self	Opposing Expression	Proper Wealth
	- Fire	**- Earth**	**- Metal**	**-Water**	**- Wood**
- Metal	Hostile Power	Hostile Resource	Friendly Self	Proper Expression	Extra Wealth

YANG WATER DAY MASTER

	+ Fire	+ Earth	+ Metal	+ Water	+ Wood
+ Water	Extra Wealth	Hostile Power	Hostile Resource	Friendly Self	Proper Expression
	- Fire	**- Earth**	**- Metal**	**- Water**	**- Wood**
+ Water	Proper Wealth	Proper Power	Proper Resource	Unfriendly Self	Opposing Expression

YIN WATER DAY MASTER

	+ Fire	+ Earth	+ Metal	+ Water	+ Wood
- Water	Proper Wealth	Proper Power	Proper Resource	Unfriendly Self	Opposing Expression
	- Fire	**- Earth**	**- Metal**	**-Water**	**- Wood**
- Water	Extra Wealth	Hostile Power	Hostile Resource	Friendly Self	Proper Expression

YANG WOOD DAY MASTER

	+ Fire	+ Earth	+ Metal	+ Water	+ Wood
+ Wood	Proper Expression	Extra Wealth	Hostile Power	Hostile Resource	Friendly Self
	- Fire	**- Earth**	**- Metal**	**-Water**	**- Wood**
+ Wood	Opposing Expression	Proper Wealth	Proper Power	Proper Resource	Unfriendly Self

YIN WOOD DAY MASTER

	+ Fire	+ Earth	+ Metal	+ Water	+ Wood
- Wood	Opposing Expression	Proper Wealth	Proper Power	Proper Resource	Unfriendly Self
	- Fire	**- Earth**	**- Metal**	**- Water**	**- Wood**
- Wood	Proper Expression	Extra Wealth	Hostile Power	Hostile Resource	Friendly Self

YANG FIRE DAY MASTER

	+ Fire	+ Earth	+ Metal	+ Water	+ Wood
+ Fire	Friendly Self	Proper Expression	Extra Wealth	Hostile Power	Hostile Resource
	- Fire	**- Earth**	**- Metal**	**- Water**	**- Wood**
+ Fire	Unfriendly Self	Opposing Expression	Proper Wealth	Proper Power	Proper Resource

YIN FIRE DAY MASTER

	+ Fire	+ Earth	+ Metal	+ Water	+ Wood
- Fire	Unfriendly Self	Opposing Expression	Proper Wealth	Proper Power	Proper Resource
	- Fire	- Earth	- Metal	- Water	- Wood
- Fire	Friendly Self	Proper Expression	Extra Wealth	Hostile Power	Hostile Resource

YANG EARTH DAY MASTER

	+ Fire	+ Earth	+ Metal	+ Water	+ Wood
+ Earth	Hostile Resource	Friendly Self	Proper Expression	Extra Wealth	Hostile Power
	- Fire	- Earth	- Metal	- Water	- Wood
+ Earth	Proper Resource	Unfriendly Self	Opposing Expression	Proper Wealth	Proper Power

YIN EARTH DAY MASTER

	+ Fire	+ Earth	+ Metal	+ Water	+ Wood
- Earth	Proper Resource	Unfriendly Self	Opposing Expression	Proper Wealth	Proper Power
	- Fire	- Earth	- Metal	- Water	- Wood
- Earth	Hostile Resource	Friendly Self	Proper Expression	Extra Wealth	Hostile Power

THE TEN DAY MASTERS AND
THE ELEMENTS REPRESENTING THEIR TEN GODS

NOTE: THE "GODS" IN ITALIC ARE THE MORE DESIRABLE ONES,
WHILE THOSE IN NORMAL TYPE ARE MORE CHALLENGING FOR YOU.

(SEE "FAMILY AND GROUP THERAPY," PAGES 59–62)

DAY MASTER	FIRE	EARTH	METAL	WATER	WOOD
-Fire	**Self** *Yin Friendly* Yang Unfriendly	**Expression** *Yin Proper* Yang Opposing	**Wealth** Yin Extra *Yang Proper*	**Power** Yin Hostile *Yang Proper*	**Resource** Yin Hostile *Yang Proper*
+Fire	**Self** Yin Unfriendly *Yang Friendly*	**Expression** Yin Opposing *Yang Proper*	**Wealth** *Yin Proper* Yang Extra	**Power** *Yin Proper* Yang Hostile	**Resource** *Yin Proper* Yang Hostile
-Earth	**Resource** Yin Hostile *Yang Proper*	**Self** *Yin Friendly* Yang Unfriendly	**Expression** *Yin Proper* Yang Opposing	**Wealth** Yin Extra *Yang Proper*	**Power** Yin Hostile *Yang Proper*
+Earth	**Resource** *Yin Proper* Yang Hostile	**Self** Yin Unfriendly *Yang Friendly*	**Expression** Yin Opposing *Yang Proper*	**Wealth** *Yin Proper* Yang Extra	**Power** *Yin Proper* Yang Hostile
-Metal	**Power** Yin Hostile *Yang Proper*	**Resource** Yin Hostile *Yang Proper*	**Self** *Yin Friendly* Yang Unfriendly	**Expression** *Yin Proper* Yang Opposing	**Wealth** Yin Extra *Yang Proper*
+Metal	**Power** *Yin Proper* Yang Hostile	**Resource** *Yin Proper* Yang Hostile	**Self** Yin Unfriendly *Yang Friendly*	**Expression** Yin Opposing *Yang Proper*	**Wealth** *Yin Proper* Yang Extra
-Water	**Wealth** Yin Extra *Yang Proper*	**Power** Yin Hostile *Yang Proper*	**Resource** Yin Hostile *Yang Proper*	**Self** *Yin Friendly* Yang Unfriendly	**Expression** *Yin Proper* Yang Opposing
+Water	**Wealth** *Yin Proper* Yang Extra	**Power** *Yin Proper* Yang Hostile	**Resource** *Yin Proper* Yang Hostile	**Self** Yin Unfriendly *Yang Friendly*	**Expression** Yin Opposing *Yang Proper*
-Wood	**Expression** *Yin Proper* Yang Opposing	**Wealth** Yin Extra *Yang Proper*	**Power** Yin Hostile *Yang Proper*	**Resource** Yin Hostile *Yang Proper*	**Self** *Yin Friendly* Yang Unfriendly
+Wood	**Expression** Yin Opposing *Yang Proper*	**Wealth** *Yin Proper* Yang Extra	**Power** *Yin Proper* Yang Hostile	**Resource** *Yin Proper* Yang Hostile	**Self** Yin Unfriendly *Yang Friendly*

THE ELEMENTS AND THEIR COLORS
(SEE "INNER ALCHEMY COLOR THERAPY," PAGES 80–82)

ELEMENT	COLORS
Fire	Red, Purple
Earth	Yellow, Beige, Brown
Metal	White, Gold, Silver, Bronze
Water	Black, Dark Blue
Wood	Green, Light Blue, Turquoise

For more on how to use the elements and their colors see the Pakua diagram, figure 7.1, on page 85.

THE BRANCHES AND THEIR ELEMENTS
(SEE "CHINESE ANIMALS—THE EARTHLY BRANCHES," PAGES 111–13)

BRANCH	MAIN ELEMENT	HIDDEN ROOTS
Rat	Yin Water	
Buffalo	Yin Earth	Yin Water, Yin Metal
Tiger	Yang Wood	Yang Fire, Yang Earth
Rabbit	Yin Wood	
Dragon	Yang Earth	Yin Wood, Yin Water
Snake	Yang Fire	Yang Earth, Yang Metal
Horse	Yin Fire	Yin Earth
Ram	Yin Earth	Yin Fire, Yin Wood
Monkey	Yang Metal	Yang Water, Yang Earth
Rooster	Yin Metal	
Dog	Yang Earth	Yin Metal, Yin Fire
Boar	Yang Water	Yang Wood

RELATIONSHIPS BETWEEN THE ANIMALS

(SEE "ANIMAL COMPATIBILITY," PAGES 114–17)

		SECRET FRIEND	ALLIES	CONFLICTS
Rat		Buffalo	Dragon, Monkey	Horse
Buffalo		Rat	Snake, Rooster	Ram
Tiger		Boar	Horse, Dog	Monkey
Rabbit		Dog	Ram, Boar	Rooster
Dragon		Rooster	Rat, Monkey	Dog
Snake		Monkey	Buffalo, Rooster	Boar
Horse		Ram	Tiger, Dog	Rat
Ram		Horse	Rabbit, Boar	Buffalo
Monkey		Snake	Rat, Dragon	Tiger

		SECRET FRIEND	ALLIES	CONFLICTS
Rooster		Dragon	Buffalo, Snake	Rabbit
Dog		Rabbit	Tiger, Horse	Dragon
Boar		Tiger	Rabbit, Ram	Snake

HOW YOUR FAMILY FITS INTO YOUR FOUR PILLARS
(SEE "UNDERSTANDING YOU AND YOUR FAMILY," PAGES 124–27)

	HOUR	DAY	MONTH	YEAR
	Children, Workers	Self, Siblings, Peers	Parents, Bosses, Upbringing	Grandparents, Society
Stem	Sons	Self	Father	Grandfather
Branch	Daughters	Marriage, Partner	Mother	Grandmother

Appendix B
Symbolic Stars

Your Inner Alchemy astrology chart includes the calculation of these exceptional stars, which are named after their particular character trait potential. They can have a positive or negative side for the bearer or others who come into contact with them. The effects will always depend on the many variables of astrology including quality and quantity of day master and other elements, and the time and place in the chart that the star occurs. Their presence helps explain degrees of impact and effects of other energies in the chart.

When they come into the chart as annual or ten-year luck (or even monthly or daily luck) then they interact with the energies in the natal chart during that period. Otherwise their position in the natal chart generally shows the area of interaction as follows:

Year branch—indicates effect on grandparents, parents, and the family in the broader sense and covers the person's childhood.

Month branch—indicates an effect on the person's young adulthood, plus on siblings and parents.

Day branch—indicates effect on their spouse or the individual's personality and life as a mature adult in his or her prime.

Hour branch—indicates effects on children or on the individual's senior years.

The Stars

Assistance Star: In a natal chart this star shows there will be help from unexpected sources thanks to the goddess Tian Yi. Disastrous situations can become fortunate; it can also enable popularity. In annual luck, this star can bring out promotion or more wealth.

Philosophy Star: Shows an interest in esoteric and philosophic matters. In your natal chart it adds a hard-working and intelligent energy, although too much of this can make for conceit.

Aggression Star: Provides potential for underlying aggression, but can either be good or bad depending on the other energies. Often ill-effects are indicated with a strong day master, but this star gives more courage to a weak day master. It can affect the person or his or her relationships.

Prospect Star: Reinforces wealth potential, but it can be an overloading force for a strong day master. For a weak day master it is mainly positive assistance.

Benevolent Star: Characterized by kindness, modesty, stability, and down-to earth qualities, it can boost a person's potential in a chart.

Kindness Star: Reinforces luck in many areas of life for most charts, such as marriage prospects, dealing with difficult events, or runs of bad luck.

Romance Star or Peach Blossom: Affects emotions, desires, charisma, relationships, marriage luck, and even career prospects due to its charismatic side. In some charts it can leave the person frustrated in relationships and more concerned with sexual conquests.

Study Star: This is an artistic star accompanied by intelligence and often is disinterested in material gains. If it reinforces similar characteristics in the chart it can well indicate excessive, reclusive behavior and is common among monks, nuns, and hermits.

Horse-Travel Star: This star means travel (traditionally by horse-back) or foreign appointments, and also movement and change. If you have more than one of these stars in your chart this could mean restlessness.

Commander Star: This star is about leadership qualities and in the natal chart would manifest as authority and presence. In annual stars it can manifest as independence and enterprising skills.

Glossary

GLOSSARY BY NUMBER

Many terms in Chinese astrology include a number as part of the term. As many of us are not familiar with Chinese, this can be particularly confusing, but the numbers are part of the proper name and we come across them continually, so to make this easier to remember we start with a short glossary by number, followed by some actual definitions of terms.

0—Wu Chi or the Nothingness: the primordial force of the universe, or the ultimate stillness. It is nothingness, no number, the time before the Big Bang.

2—Yin and Yang: "then the One became Two," from ancient Taoist legends. Yin and yang are opposites—if yin is dark, yang is light, etc.

3—Three Pure Ones: can be seen as the highest gods in Taoism. It is an expression used to represent other trinities in Taoist theory. See figure 1.1 on page 6.

3—Cosmic Trinity: heaven luck, earth luck, and human luck. Three is a magic number in many religions, and these three lucks in astrology are always interdependent.

4—Four Pillars: another name for Chinese astrology. Also the birth data used in astrology. Reading the chart from right to left are the year pillar, month pillar, day pillar, and hour pillar.

5—Five Elements: Wood, Fire, Earth, Metal, and Water. The five energies that are the building blocks of the universe. They are components of all things, tangible and intangible, with specific energies, correlations to many things and characteristics. They exist in a never-ending cycle of transformation and change, decline and regeneration.

5—**Five Phases:** self, expression, wealth, power, resource. These are the five areas of life defined by the elements.

6—**Healing Sounds:** an Inner Alchemy practice to balance energy. The six sounds are Fire, Earth, Metal, Water, Wood, and Triple Heater.

8—**Eight Forces:** fire, earth, lake and rain, heaven, water, mountain, thunder, and wind. They are expressed as the trigrams on the pakua.

8—**Eight Trigrams of the Pakua:** an expression of the eight natural forces of the universe listed above. When chanting them as part of the Inner Alchemy practices the order goes: Kan, Li, Gen, Tui, Kun, Ken, Xun, Chen.

8—**Ba Zi:** characters of the birth chart. It is another name for the method of four pillars Chinese astrology used in this book. It literally means eight characters, which are the eight parts of the birth chart if we divide the four pillars into two—the heavenly stems on the top lines and the earthly branches on the lower lines.

10—**Ten Gods:** the yin and yang versions of the five phases adapted according to the day master—self, unfriendly self, proper expression, opposing expression, proper wealth, extra wealth, proper power, hostile power, proper resource, hostile resource.

10—**Heavenly Stems:** the cycle of energies from the heavens, the yin and yang aspects of the elements used to count heavenly time—Yang Wood, Yin Wood, Yang Fire, Yin Fire, Yang Earth, Yin Earth, Yang Metal, Yin Metal, Yang Water, Yin Water.

10—**Ten-Year Luck Periods:** the dynamic part of the chart. Significant energies coming in for ten-year periods in the form of a heavenly stem and earthly branch pillar. They can explain why people's lives change suddenly.

12—**Earthly Branches:** the Taoist way to count time on Earth, marking a twelve-year cycle but also the cycle of the months, seasons, directions, and hours. Expressed as the twelve animals, in order: Rat, Ox, Tiger, Rabbit, Dragon, Snake, Horse, Sheep, Monkey, Rooster, Dog, and Pig.

GLOSSARY BY TERM

Children's Palace: one of the four pillars on your birth chart. This aspect of your chart is obtained from the hour of birth; it is the first pillar when reading from the left. It represents your relationship with your children, employees, and your life in your senior years.

Day Master: the element that represents one's self in your birth chart, found in the top, or heavenly stem, line of the day pillar.

Grandparents' Palace: this aspect of your chart is the year pillar on the far right of birth chart. It indicates the relationship of the day master to grandparents, as well as to society in a broader sense.

Marriage Palace: This is the day branch, found under the day master on the day pillar. It describes the day master's marriage partner and also siblings, showing how the day master views marriage and actual expectations for it.

Pakua: the diagram of the natural forces of the universe. It is an octagon with eight trigrams representing the eight forces of nature in their eight geographical directions. It is read from the center outward.

Parents' Palace: the month pillar on the birth chart, second from the right. It describes the relationship with parents, upbringing, and education.

Peach Blossom: a love interest or potential love attraction.

Predominant Heavenly Influence: this aspect of your chart is obtained from the month branch; this is a phase that motivates your life more than the other four phases.

# Recommended Reading

Taoist Practices

All of Mantak Chia's books on the Universal Healing Tao practices are based on the Taoist view of the universe, using the yin, yang, and five-element theory. After having read this book and explored your own five-element makeup, you might particularly like to read or re-read the following books by Mantak Chia:

Emotional Wisdom (essential entry-level book for under-standing Inner Alchemy practices)
Transform Your Stress into Vitality (essential entry-level book for understanding Inner Alchemy practices)
Healing Light of the Tao
Taoist Cosmic Healing and *Taoist Astral Healing*
Wisdom Chi Kung
Golden Elixir Chi Kung
The Alchemy of Sexual Energy
Cosmic Fusion, Fusion of the Five Elements, and *Fusion of the Eight Psychic Channels*
The Taoist Soul Body
Sealing of the Five Senses

You can also find an Inner Alchemy practices class or instructor in your country and booklet versions of the texts listed above by looking on the Universal Healing Tao website.

Five-Element Nutrition

The Tao of Delicious by Mantak Chia and Shashi Solluna
Cosmic Nutrition by Mantak Chia

Taoist or Chinese Astrology

Five Element Chinese Astrology Made Easy by David Twicken
Treasures of Tao by David Twicken
Four Pillars and Oriental Medicine by David Twicken

For a serious study of the subject, understanding the very weighty calculations necessary to do the charting is a necessary step, but if you just want to know a little bit more then start with:

The Complete Idiot's Guide to Feng Shui, Third Edition by Elizabeth Moran, Master Joseph Yu, and Master Val Biktashev

Although essentially a guide to feng shui (and really the best guide to real feng shui for the general public, highly praised, and read by professionals) the second part of this book is on astrology and is a very good introduction.

Master Joseph Yu—an eminent feng shui master—also has an excellent correspondence course backed up by a vibrant Yahoo private discussion list where the student can study, discuss charts, and be mentored by more experienced members of this online community.

The following books discuss Chinese astrology from the basic level of animals:

The Chinese Astrology Bible by Derek Walters, who is also the author of the very intense *The Complete Guide to Chinese Astrology*
Cosmic Astrology by Mantak Chia and William U. Wei—a comprehensive reference volume integrating Western and Eastern systems

Chinese Medicine and Acupuncture
(an interesting diversion and a deep, relevant path)

The Complete Stems and Branches: Time and Space in Traditional Acupuncture by Roisin Golding

The Yellow Emperor's Classic of Medicine—there are many translations of this ancient Chinese classic

Dragon Rises, Red Bird Flies: Psychology and Chinese Medicine by Leon Hammer

Between Heaven and Earth: A Guide to Chinese Medicine by Harriet Beinfield and Efrem Korngold

The Web That Has No Weaver: Understanding Chinese Medicine by Ted J. Kaptchuk

Wood Becomes Water: Chinese Medicine in Everyday Life by Gail Reichstein

Massage Therapies (based on Taoist five-element theory)

Chi Nei Tsang, Advanced Chi Nei Tsang, and *Karsai Nei Tsang* by Mantak Chia

Five Elements, Six Conditions: A Taoist Approach to Emotional Healing, Psychology, and Internal Alchemy by Gilles Marin (see also Gilles Marin's Chi Nei Tsang books)

Taoist Thought

The Secret Teachings of the Tao Te Ching by Mantak Chia and Tau Huang

The Secret and Sublime: Taoist Mysteries and Magic by John Blofeld

Planets and Solar System

The Planets by Dava Sobel

Earth Energies

The New View over Atlantis by John Michell

About the Authors

MANTAK CHIA

Mantak Chia has been studying the Taoist approach to life since childhood. His mastery of this ancient knowledge, enhanced by his study of other disciplines, has resulted in the development of the Universal Healing Tao system, which is now being taught throughout the world.

Mantak Chia was born in Thailand to Chinese parents in 1944. When he was six years old, he learned from Buddhist monks how to sit and "still the mind." While in grammar school he learned traditional Thai boxing, and he soon went on to acquire considerable skill in aikido, yoga, and Tai Chi. His studies of the Taoist way of life began in earnest when he was a student in Hong Kong, ultimately leading to his mastery of a wide variety of esoteric disciplines, with the guidance of several masters, including Master Yi Eng (I Yun) Master Meugi, Master Cheng Yao Lun, and Master Pan Yu. To better understand the mechanisms behind healing energy, he also studied Western anatomy and medical sciences.

Master Chia has taught his system of healing and energizing practices to tens of thousands of students and trained more than two thousand instructors and practitioners throughout the world. He has established centers for Taoist study and training in many countries around the globe. In June of 1990, he was honored by the International Congress of Chinese Medicine and Qi Gong (Chi Kung), which named him the Qi Gong Master of the Year.

CHRISTINE HARKNESS-GILES

Christine Harkness-Giles is a certified instructor in the Universal Healing Tao system and a teaching feng shui consultant. She was born in the United Kingdom. She has been a student of Taoism for many years, studying feng shui, Chinese astrology, and the I Ching, notably with Master Joseph Yu, founder of the Feng Shui Research Centre (FSRC). She promotes these Taoist arts in Europe through the Feng Shui Research Center world network, which is dedicated to teaching, consulting, research, and providing information on authentic Taoist methods.

Meeting Mantak Chia and learning the Inner Alchemy practices provided the "missing link" for her between Taoist knowledge and living Taoist philosophy in today's world, a natural way to live in harmony with the environment. Working with chi and feeling chi in the body encouraged her to become a UHT instructor to pass on the teaching.

She regularly assisted Mantak Chia as a translator during his astrology consultations. These remarkable readings were, for Christine as an astrologer, "master classes" in Mantak Chia's own Inner Alchemy astrology, revealing true insights into the five-element makeup of a person combined with techniques for enhancing their chi. She uses Inner Alchemy astrology with her students, fellow instructors, and feng shui clients as well as teaching the method at home in the Eurostar triangle of London, Paris, and Brussels, as well as in Hawaii.

The Universal Healing Tao System and Training Center

THE UNIVERSAL HEALING TAO SYSTEM

The ultimate goal of Taoist practice is to transcend physical boundaries through the development of the soul and the spirit within the human. That is also the guiding principle behind the Universal Healing Tao, a practical system of self-development that enables individuals to complete the harmonious evolution of their physical, mental, and spiritual bodies. Through a series of ancient Chinese meditative and internal energy exercises, the practitioner learns to increase physical energy, release tension, improve health, practice self-defense, and gain the ability to heal him- or herself and others. In the process of creating a solid foundation of health and well-being in the physical body, the practitioner also creates the basis for developing his or her spiritual potential by learning to tap in to the natural energies of the sun, moon, earth, stars, and other environmental forces.

The Universal Healing Tao practices are derived from ancient techniques rooted in the processes of nature. They have been gathered and integrated into a coherent, accessible system for well-being that works directly with the life force, or chi, that flows through the meridian system of the body.

Master Chia has spent years developing and perfecting techniques for teaching these traditional practices to students around the world through ongoing classes, workshops, private instruction, and healing sessions, as well as books and video and audio products. Further information can be obtained at www.universal-tao.com.

THE UNIVERSAL HEALING TAO TRAINING CENTER

The Tao Garden Resort and Training Center in northern Thailand is the home of Master Chia and serves as the worldwide headquarters for Universal Healing Tao activities. This integrated wellness, holistic health, and training center is situated on eighty acres surrounded by the beautiful Himalayan foothills near the historic walled city of Chiang Mai. The serene setting includes flower and herb gardens ideal for meditation, open-air pavilions for practicing Chi Kung, and a health and fitness spa.

The center offers classes year round, as well as summer and winter retreats. It can accommodate two hundred students, and group leasing can be arranged. For information on courses, books, products, and other resources, see below.

RESOURCES

Universal Healing Tao Center
274 Moo 7, Luang Nua, Doi Saket, Chiang Mai, 50220 Thailand
Tel: (66)(53) 495-596 Fax: (66)(53) 495-852
E-mail: universaltao@universal-tao.com
Web site: www.universal-tao.com

For information on retreats and the health spa, contact:
Tao Garden Health Spa & Resort
E-mail: info@tao-garden.com, taogarden@hotmail.com
Web site: www.tao-garden.com

Good Chi • Good Heart • Good Intention

Index

Page numbers in *italics* refer to illustrations and tables.

BOOKS OF RELATED INTEREST

Cosmic Astrology

An East-West Guide to Your Internal Energy Persona

by Mantak Chia and William U. Wei

Cosmic Detox

A Taoist Approach to Internal Cleansing

by Mantak Chia and William U. Wei

Cosmic Nutrition

The Taoist Approach to Health and Longevity

by Mantak Chia and William U. Wei

Cosmic Fusion

The Inner Alchemy of the Eight Forces

by Mantak Chia

The Alchemy of Sexual Energy

Connecting to the Universe from Within

by Mantak Chia

Healing Love through the Tao

Cultivating Female Sexual Energy

by Mantak Chia

Taoist Shaman

Practices from the Wheel of Life

by Mantak Chia and Kris Deva North

Simple Chi Kung

Exercises for Awakening the Life-Force Energy

by Mantak Chia and Lee Holden

INNER TRADITIONS • BEAR & COMPANY
P.O. Box 388
Rochester, VT 05767
1-800-246-8648
www.InnerTraditions.com

Or contact your local bookseller